contents

Introduction

Everyone who has picked up this book to read will have an inherent interest in creativity. It is an intriguing, illusive subject, intangible and exciting. It embodies the essence of the unknown, of genius, of our inspiration and motivation to get the most out of life. And yet how do we become creative? Most artists would consider themselves to be creative but creativity is not exclusively an artistic property. Many books exploring creativity have focused on scientists' discoveries and engineers' innovations and inventions. Industry has realised the potential of creativity in their employees and many companies now train their graduates in creative thinking. Rolls-Royce became so inspired by their innovators that they have recently increased training of their graduates in this area. An example of one such innovation is given in the photograph shown here, of the nose spinner of the Rolls-Royce aero-engine. The problem to solve was two-fold. It would be a weight saving to replace the metal nose with glass reinforced plastic. However, the nose was subject to frosting and if the part was made of an insulating material it could not be thermally de-iced. The solution, dreamt up overnight in a classic case of 'incubation', was to make the tip out of rubber, which simply bent over and lost its frosty load at a critical rotational speed. It was then as good as new! This was a huge saving in problem solving time as well as component parts.

What is creativity? The Western concept seems to relate it to an observable product whereas the Eastern concept seems to involve a state of personal fulfilment, the expression of the inner essence (Lubart in Sternberg, 1999). Despite its sense of intrigue, it holds with it a very un-measurable quality and scientists have stayed away from studying such an untouchable subject. Sternberg (1999) has recently collected together most of the latest ideas on creativity in his 'Handbook of creativity'. He states that between 1975 to 1994 only 0.5% of the entries in psychological abstracts showed an entry relating to creativity, compared with 1.5% on reading. Sternberg suggests that there are six reasons for this lack of activity. These are: the sense of mysticism surrounding creativity; that it lacks in theory; that there is no clear definition; that it is not mainstream psychology; that it is considered an extraordinary version of the ordinary; it has been viewed in a unidisciplinary manner and only part of it has been studied at any one time because it is multidisciplinary in nature. All of this, however, seems to add fuel to the fire of those interested in the matter. The challenge after reviewing all the available studies to date, is to find answers to the following (Mayer in Sternberg, 1999):

What is creativity?
Is creativity a property of products or processes or people?
Is creativity a personal or social phenomenon?
Is creativity common to all people or a unique characteristic of a select few?

Courtesy Rolls-Royce plc.

Is creativity a domain-general activity that is essentially the same in all contexts or a domain-specific activity that depends on the context under consideration?
Is creativity best conceived as a set of characteristics along which people may vary or as uniquely manifested in each creative individual?

Creativity can be regarded as an emerging 'multidisciplinary' discipline.

In this small and unpretentious book, we attempt not to give you tips to become creative but to focus on five cases of individuals who have tried to inspire their students or graduates to become creative in different contexts. The case studies focused on the art, design, science, engineering and industry. We have explored what it is about what they do, which helps the students realise their potential. Their experiences offer simple and yet clear and very useful guidelines to follow if you are attempting to set up a course which helps to foster a student's or an employee's creativity. The book is the outcome of a DfEE funded project, 'Fostering creativity within engineering' and is largely intended to help engineering educators develop learning situations in which their students' creativity is encouraged. It becomes obvious, however, that as creativity is such a multidisciplinary, or perhaps 'non-disciplinary' subject, that most of the book applies to any degree subject or any other learning situation.

The book has been organised in a surprisingly traditional fashion for such a subject, with an initial consultation of the literature regarding the latest ideas on what creativity might be; who has studied it (from which perspective); what processes are thought to occur in the act of being creative and what techniques are available to develop creative potential.

This is followed by a presentation of the five case studies in a fairly similar format, describing what the organisers have done and what guidelines arise for facilitating the emergence of creativity. We present a model, which demonstrates how each case promotes certain parts of the path towards an innovation, from an idea in a person's head. It is intended that each case may be traced within the model, as well as indicating the blocks which impede the process and the conditions which aid it. A final section demonstrates more fully what principles emerge to help to foster creativity within any course.

Despite the traditional ordering at the macro level, it is intended that the book becomes a study of process and content of creativity. Hence at a micro level, it is presented in a way which is intended to help you reflect upon some of the concepts. They are rarely linear ideas and cannot therefore be represented as such. At one level we might imagine that we are part of the creative process, as the researcher of the cases. We might consider the creative process involved in the development of courses to foster creativity – as shown in the model, where individual cases are tracked. At yet another level, we can think of the creative process in which the students have been involved on the courses; or as the reader, developing a base of knowledge about creativity and courses to foster creativity and incubating the ideas until a new way of teaching your own course emerges...

The development of creative alternatives in decision problems
(CLEMEN, 1996)

The making of the new and the rearranging of the old
(BENTLEY, 1997)

The process of generating unique products by transformation of existing products. These products, tangible and intangible, must be unique only to the creator, and must meet the criteria of purpose and value established by the creator.
(WELSCH IN ISAKSEN *ET AL*, 1993)

In a creative act of perception one first becomes aware (generally non verbally) of a new set of relevant differences and one begins to feel out or note a new set of similarities which do not come merely from past knowledge.
(BOHM, 1998)

The achieving of tangible products such as works of art or science
(ABRA, 1997)

An unease emerging out of a struggle between two opposing forces
(ROBINSON / RUNDELL, 1994)

The process of becoming sensitive to problems, deficiencies, gaps in knowledge, missing elements, disharmonies, and so on; identifying the difficult; searching for solutions, making guesses or formulating hypotheses about the deficiencies, testing and retesting them and finally communicating the results
(TORRANCE, IN ISAKSEN *ET AL*, 1993)

A creative person can regularly solve problems or can fashion products ranging from a theory to a new technique in a domain in a way that is ultimately judged acceptable (although initially it may seem bizarre) by the field; in this case the field is a cultural setting of people and institutions that make judgements about new products in a domain.
(GARDNER IN RUSSELL, 1998)

The ability to perceive reality accurately and compare cultures objectively, having a genuine degree of spontaneity and being able to look at things in a fresh, simple, naïve way.
(DAVIS IN CLEMEN, 1996)

Someone is creative if knowledgeable individuals agree
(AMABILE IN ABRA, 1997)

Conceptual combination – merging of two or more concepts resulting in a novel entity
(WARD *ET AL*, 1997)

Creativity is a process needed for problem solving. Secondly creativity is not a special gift enjoyed by a few but a common ability possessed by most people which can be developed or suppressed as a result of their individual experiences.
(JONES IN ISAKSEN *ET AL*, 1993)

Improbabilist creativity – new and valued creativity within constraints Impossibilist – transformation of conceptual space – new ideas arise that were impossible before
(BODEN, 1996)

Novel associations which are useful
(ISAKSEN AND TREFFINGER IN ISAKSEN *ET AL*, 1993)

Defining creativity

What is creativity? Can we define what we are looking for? Often people are careful not to define creativity as such, as it is such a complex phenomenon. Furthermore, teaching creativity becomes fostering, nurturing, stimulating or allowing creativity.

Creativity studies, rather than having one universal definition, contain a variety of definitions, theories, and assessment approaches involving process, ability and awareness. Despite the apparent confusion and contradictions resulting from uses of multiple definitions, some degree of agreement has been identified.

A working definition

The necessity for an appropriate definition for this project has lead us to construct a working definition as follows: ***Creativity is shared imagination.***

'Imagination' as novel (rather than visual) memory and individual or personal. 'Shared' in the sense that the audience becomes part of it. Through the medium of communication and filters of perception, the audience reconstructs the person's intention in their imagination. A person can relate to an audience, although sharing is more than communicating, hearing or seeing. It is making an audience aware of a novel, personal visualisation, processed by associative incubation of the individual. Creativity becomes innovative when a commercial application becomes apparent. If the creativity is not domain specific it becomes an invention.

Approaches to studying creativity

Problem solving and decision making – many studies have developed with the aim of improving problem solving in engineering and decision making in management.
(Finke *et al*, 1992, Clemen, 1996)

Behaviourist theories
Creative behaviour is seen as a conglomerate of responses to environmental stimuli
(Maltzmann, Skinner in Clemen, 1996)

Psychometric
These approaches test individuals for their way of thinking and relate these to creative abilities eg. tendency towards convergent or divergent thinking
(Eysenck in Boden, 1996)

Artificial intelligence – Recent studies on the mimicry of human processes and the extension of these using computers. They assume structured rather than random associations
(Boden, 1996)

Biographical
Studies of how creativity has been developed in artists and scientists with particular talent or 'genius'. 'The student of creativity must reconstruct the mental life of the creative individual at various points in the development of his work and study genetic, familial, motivational and environmental factors.'
(Gruber in Gardner, 1982)

Pragmatic approaches
Common approaches which involve many years of study to develop techniques which have been implemented and shown to work , to develop creativity in individuals or groups.
(Finke *et al*, 1992)

Leadership – there are often links between creativity and leadership and creative leadership has become a study in its own right
(Simonton in Sternberg, 1997)

Psychoanalytical theories
Creativity is considered to be the result of preconscious mental activity
(Kris, Kubie, Rugg in Clemen, 1996)

Multiple components approach

These studies use the 'Investment theory', that creativity involves many aspects including: intellectual processes, knowledge structures, intellectual style, personality traits, motivational factors, environmental context (STERNBERG AND LUBART IN FINKE *ET AL* 1992)

Sociological/historical –

Studies concerned with the social, environmental and cultural effects on creativity (AMABILE, SIMONTON IN FINKE *ET AL*, 1992)

The cognitive approach

Cognitive models have become more abundant since the 1980s. Before then creativity was considered to be too 'unscientific' for cognitive science. (GILHOOLY, 1997)

Creative visualisations

Approaches to the study of how creativity is developed using imagery – people can mentally synthesise simple visual forms to make unexpected creative discoveries. (FINKE *ET AL*, 1992)

The cognitive approach has developed from a variety of conceptions of creative thinking; a random association of ideas, a juxtaposition of two previously unrelated thoughts, chance configuration of ideas, evolution of ideas, the transformation of conceptual space, magic synthesis, selective combination of ideas, illumination... All of these conceptions of creative cognition stress the association of ideas into new, larger, meaningful complexes of ideas. As research in cognitive psychology has been limited, most of the creative techniques, based on underlying creative processes are not derived from cognitive models but have developed in a pragmatic manner. (Gilhooly, 1997, Finke *et al*, 1992, Ward *et al*, 1995, Ward *et al*, 1997, Koestler, 1989, Boden, 1996, Isaksen *et al*, 1993).

Creative potential

Are there creative types of people who have certain intelligence, knowledge, technical skills, special talents and values? What about environmental conditions - politico-religious factors, cultural factors, socio-economic factors and educational factors? Does a creative person have a particular personality – internal motivation, confidence, non-conformity, good self image, being emotional, perceptual and open to new ideas (Boden, Jones in Isaksen *et al*, 1993)? In this section we review some of the conditions which have been shown to hinder or foster creativity.

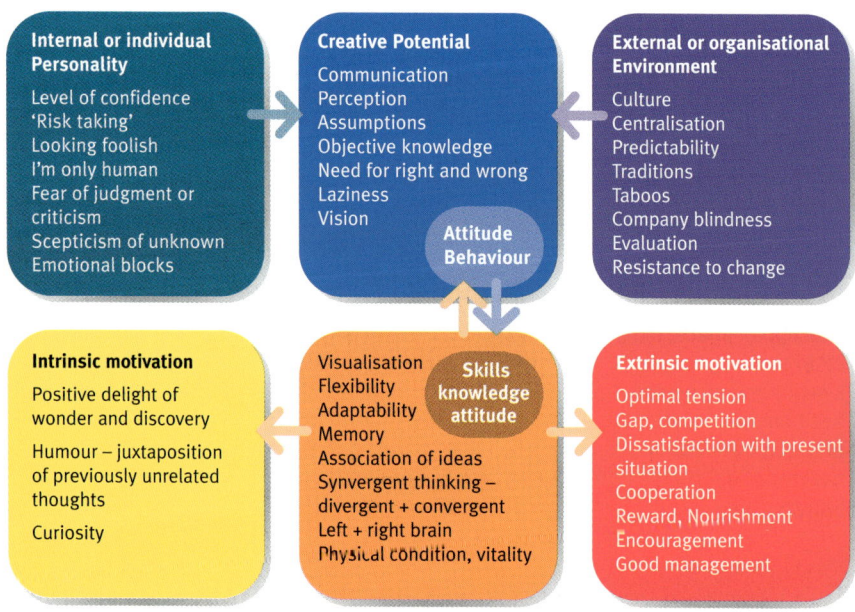

Internal or individual Personality

Level of confidence
'Risk taking'
Looking foolish
I'm only human
Fear of judgment or criticism
Scepticism of unknown
Emotional blocks

Creative Potential

Communication
Perception
Assumptions
Objective knowledge
Need for right and wrong
Laziness
Vision

Attitude Behaviour

External or organisational Environment

Culture
Centralisation
Predictability
Traditions
Taboos
Company blindness
Evaluation
Resistance to change

Intrinsic motivation

Positive delight of wonder and discovery

Humour – juxtaposition of previously unrelated thoughts

Curiosity

Visualisation
Flexibility
Adaptability
Memory
Association of ideas
Synvergent thinking – divergent + convergent
Left + right brain
Physical condition, vitality

Skills knowledge attitude

Extrinsic motivation

Optimal tension
Gap, competition
Dissatisfaction with present situation
Cooperation
Reward, Nourishment
Encouragement
Good management

The figure above shows how the various obstacles and conditions leading towards a creative output are linked.

The green box shows the internal aspects of the individual. These may be brought about by psychological conditions and are the inner shell of the egg shown in the illustration. Obviously the block or obstacle is the converse of the condition leading towards creativity. For instance, a high level of confidence in ability will help and a low level will hinder.

The blue box shows the conditions or obstacles which might help or hinder creativity, from an external perspective. These are the outer shell of our egg illustration.

These two boxes will influence the blue box , which is the creative potential of the individual. In this box the person's ability to communicate their ideas, to see the possibilities in a situation, and to acknowledge assumptions will depend upon their own conditioning and their environment.

The yellow box shows the intrinsic motivation for creativity, which may be set up directly by the individual personality in the green box.

The red box is the extrinsic motivation which may be set up directly from the external environment given in purple.

However, under less advantageous situations where the obstacles have become insurmountable, the creative potential needs to be aided by certain skills, knowledge and awareness, shown in the orange box. These might be the ability to visualise what one wants to do, to think laterally as well as vertically, to associate different sets of ideas and so on. It appears to be possible to develop the creative potential and to take a back route towards the extrinsic or the intrinsic motivation via development of these areas. Even a negative environment, given the right sort of attitude, can be a motivation towards creative change, if the individual sees it as an opportunity for improvement.

Internal or individual personality

"Every act of creation is first an act of destruction."

PABLO PICASSO

Some people assume there are those who are creative and those who are not. This proposal has been discussed by researchers and authors from a variety of disciplines and yet there appears to be no real evidence to this effect, although the research is in its early stages. It is therefore assumed that there is a creative potential , which everyone can develop, and some are more able to draw on this than others. Certain psychological profiles and personality types seem more intrinsically able to draw on this whilst others need some help. There is some evidence that creative people have undergone an intense experience of some kind which helps them to develop a different awareness (Eysenck, 1996). Fairly rigorous studies have shown a high relationship between certain qualities in a person which tend to be associated with their creative ability. For example, psychometric testing is often used to 'objectify' a creative type. Tests of 'origence' indicate independence of attitude and social behaviour, dominance, introversion, openness to stimuli, wide interests, self acceptance, intuition, asocial behaviour, unconcern for social norms, radicalism

and rejection of external controls – and these match high levels of creativity (Eysenck, 1996). However, it is accepted that the need for dominance and asocial behaviour may have been necessary in order to combat an obstructive environment and need not be a prerequisite!

'When you think you can or you can't, you'll prove yourself correct.'

HENRY FORD

As shown in the egg illustration, a major barrier to creativity is the **lack of confidence** or belief in one's ability. Most connected with fear, discussed below, this avoids risk taking (Bentley, 1997), looking foolish, and so on. One of the most common excuses when faced with problems or mistakes is *'Well, what do you want? **I'm only human'***. This 'human barrier' has been studied in depth:

'We can show that each of the ten billion neurons in the human brain has a possibility of connections of one with twenty-eight noughts after it! If a single neuron has this quality of potential, we can hardly imagine what the whole brain can do. What it means is that the total number of possible combinations/permutations in the brain, if written out, would be 1 followed by 10.5 million kilometres of noughts!'

'No human yet exists who can use all the potential of his brain. This is why we don't accept any pessimistic estimates of the limits of the human brain. It is unlimited!'

(ANOKHIN IN BUZAN, 1999)

Furthermore, **the fear of judgment or criticism**, the fear of taking a risk (Clemen, 1996), the **scepticism or intolerance of the unknown** (Bentley, 1997) presents an **emotional barrier** to creative thinking. As shown in the egg illustration, breaking the shell requires courage, it will allow others to judge the broken pieces. Breaking away from fear requires self-belief, as shown when Nelson Mandela addressed South Africa in 1994:

Our deepest fear is not that we are inadequate. Our deepest fear is that we are powerful beyond measure. It is our light, not our darkness that most frightens us. We ask ourselves "who am I to be brilliant, gorgeous, talented, fabulous?" Actually, who are you not to be? You are a child of God. Your playing small doesn't serve the world. There's nothing enlightened about shrinking so that other people won't feel insecure around you. We are all meant to shine as children do... And as we let our own light shine, we unconsciously give other people permission to do the same. As we are liberated from our own fear, our presence automatically liberates others...

Creative potential

'True creativity starts where language ends.'

KOESTLER, 1989

Looking more closely at the creative potential discussed above, we need to explore those attitudes and behaviours which characterise those who utilise this potential best. As creativity may be looked upon as 'shared imagination' one needs to communicate in some way while creating. Bohm (1998) points out that "because people cannot communicate their ideas, they assume their perceptions are private and subjective.' When the individual communicates his or her imagination, conceptual and perceptual barriers become apparent.

Communication requires mutual understanding of a way of thinking which will depend upon a similar knowledge base. Despite this, knowledge can prevent creative ideas from growing. 'Creativity presents us with a paradox; knowledge is essential for creativity yet an automatic adherence to knowledge can blind you to creative ideas' (Ward *et al*, 1995). 'The individual needs to diverge from common knowledge, guiding his or her audience that is after all expecting a **right or wrong** answer. Creativity lies in the grey areas' (Bentley, 1997). Creativity, therefore has to move us away from the need for **objective** knowledge.

"The real magic lies, not in seeing new landscapes but in having new eyes.'
MARCEL PROUST IN GELB, 1996

We focus on what we know and recognise what is familiar, we match to our memory and **assume** the rest. Koestler (1989) calls this 'snow-blindness or mental eye cataract'. **Perception**, therefore, often follows purpose but with new associations, perception expands (Gelb, 1996). Perceptual blocks may be stereotyping, tacit assumptions, inability to understand a problem at different levels, inability to see a problem from another's perspective (Clemen, 1996), an 'enslavement to the stock conceptions due to **laziness** and appetite for simplicity in visual perception' (McKim, 1980). Breaking away from this natural tendency towards stereotyped **vision** requires effort.

'Part of what we perceive comes through our senses from the object before us, another part (and it may be the larger part) always comes out of our mind' (James in McKim, 1980).

We tend to think, beginning with a single perceptual pattern and then proceed immediately to delve deeply into that pattern for a solution. DeBono (in COCD, 1999) describes this as vertical thinking. Thinking that generates alternative ways of seeing the pattern of a problem before seeking a solution, he calls lateral thinking. The creative thinker will recentre their perception (think laterally) of the same problem by regrouping it into a variety of problems (McKim, 1980). Recentring vision becomes the fundamental experience in 'unlearning'.

'Our capacity to see, hear, touch, taste, and smell is shrouded... that an intensive discipline of unlearning is necessary for anyone before one can begin to experience the world afresh, with innocence, truth and love' (Laing in McKim 1980).

External or organisational environment

In the egg illustration, the individual experiences an inner (personal) and an outer (environmental) barrier. Special effort is required within academia and industry to create that necessary creative **culture**. As Adams points out, 'the natural tendency of organisations to routinise, decrease uncertainty, increase **predictability**, and **centralise** functions and controls is certainly at odds with creativity' (Adams in Clemen, 1996). Environmental barriers include time, rewards, **tradition, taboos,** competition, **company blindness** and **summative evaluation**. In general all institutions show severe resistance to change. The more innovative the action the more **resistance** may be expected, 'a new idea always brings the need of abundance of the old' (Gelb, 1996).

The environment must be suitable, must support and reward creative ideas (Russell, 1998), be safe and allow risk-taking. 'It's easier to ask for forgiveness than permission. Many ideas rot on the vine waiting for permission' (Gelb, 1996).

Does there need to be a good, supportive, nurturing environment to breed creativity? 'Mozart grew up surrounded by magnificent music. Newton took every opportunity to immerse himself physically and intellectually in light' (Gelb, 1996). Abra (1997) certainly suggests that in order to nurture creativity, a hothouse environment is needed: stimulation, reinforcement, persistence, recognition, respect, setting oneself apart, potential attention and approval, dedication and importance.

Extrinsic and intrinsic motivation

Although most creative work is driven from the delight of **wonder and discovery**, there is some evidence that extrinsic motivation can lead towards more creative results (Abra, 1997). He proposes a model whereby a 'non specific' multi-motivated energy pool is created which originates from many different sources.

Creativity can be motivated extrinsically or intrinsically, and is related to freedom, self motivation, sufficient resources, **encouragement**, recognition, sufficient time, **good project management** and good organisation climate (Hohn, 1998).

'Truly creative people are most attracted by the nourishment afforded by the internal carrot and relatively less motivated by external rewards and fear'
McKim, 1980

It is also suggested that despite the need for a 'hothouse' environment people can benefit from being placed in an optimal tension zone rather than in a safe relaxed haven in order to be motivated to create. Gestalt psychology theory proposes that all problem solving/creative acts begin with a **gap** or tension. Perkins (in Sternberg, 1997) proposes that **dissatisfaction** at the aesthetic level with an existing situation motivates creativity. Creativity is seen as operating on the boundaries within which we have been thinking.

There is further debate as to whether **cooperation** or **competition** is better for motivating creativity. Some say competition is inevitable, productive, enjoyable and builds character. Kohn would disagree with this and proposes cooperation is better and reinforcement is reciprocal and more likely to lead to creativity (Abra, 1997).

'Humour is the tenderness of fear.'

GUILLERMO MORDILLO

Finally we come to humour – the best motivator on earth. 'Reason and logic oppose humour and fantasy' (Clemen, 1996). 'A uniquely human way to reduce tension and return to optimal tension is to laugh' (McKim, 1980). 'Humour echoes and supports the process of creative thinking. The essence of humour is a shift of expectation, a juxtaposition of previously unrelated elements. Haha is the first cousin of aha!' (Gelb, 1996). Koestler (1989) also describes creativity as the juxtaposition of the three aspects of a triptych containing humour, discovery or knowledge and art or feeling and emotion.

Skills, knowledge, attitude

'Everything has been accomplished because somebody pictured it.'

GELB, 1996

In this box, we are proposing certain knowledge, abilities and ways of thinking that will help to develop the motivation and potential to create. The ability to visualise an idea is critical. The visual vehicle with its ability to facilitate holistic, spatial, metaphorical and transformational operations provides a vital and creative complement to reasoning (McKim, 1980). 'Most of us do it unconsciously and in a negative fashion. It's called worrying, ie. psychophysical preparation to failure. Instead conscious creative **visualisation** generates positive results, preparing for success' (Gelb, 1996).

The use of pre-inventive forms to develop creative visualisations are described by Ward *et al* (1995) and are used to give rise to creative cognition, novel visual patterns and object forms which aid divergent thought. Visualisation starts from perception through different filters (McKim, 1980). The variety of ideas results from the ability to change from one imaginative filter to another, the key concept is **flexibility** or **adaptability** (Clemen, 1996; McKim, 1980).

'Memory confers both the freedom to break from accepted wisdom, and the power to create the new.'

RAYMOND KEENE, CHESS GRANDMASTER IN GELB, 1996

Memory appears to be another important ability for creativity. Studies regarding memory have shown that there are great parallels between memory and creativity. This at first sight seems to conflict with education theory which proposes that experiencing learning as memory is one of the lowest descriptions in the hierarchy of learning and seeing. Learning as being creative would be the highest (Baillie and Hession, 1998, Bowden and Marton, 1998). However, it is recognised that to be creative a good memory of previously learnt knowledge is crucial. Furthermore, the more associative the thinking, the more creative it is and the better it is memorised. 'The more a fact is **associated** within the mind, the better possession of it our memory retains, each of its associates becomes a hook on which it hangs, a means to fish it up, when sunk beneath the surface. Together they form a network of attachments by which it is woven in the entire tissue of our thought' (James in Gelb, 1996).

'The secret of a good memory is thus the secret of forming diverse and multiple associations with every fact we care to retain. It is suggested that the best way of making powerful association is imaginary, the more absurd, unusual, colourful, multi-sensory the better to retain' (Gelb, 1996).

'Zeus, the king of the gods, spent nine days and nine nights making passionate love to Mnemosyne, the goddess of memory, a coupling which resulted in the birth of the nine muses. The muses represent creativity. So according to the myth, applying energy or power to memory produces a fertilisation, which results in creativity'

BUZAN, 1999

There is also much discussion in the literature about left and right brain thinking. It is now widely acknowledged that we can learn how to use the less developed part of our brains. The left hemisphere, associated with the right hand, deals with discipline, logic, objectivity, reason, judgement, knowledge, skill and language: developing, expressing and realising ideas, to bring in a world of action (McKim, 1980). The right hemisphere, associated with the left hand, deals with openness, receptivity, subjectivity, playfulness, feeling, motivation, sensory and imaginative processes (McKim, 1980). The left hemisphere and right hemisphere have been associated with **convergent** and **divergent** thinking. Convergent thinking is the search for one answer, whereas divergent thinking means production of alternative solutions to a problem; a broader, more flexible and open search process.

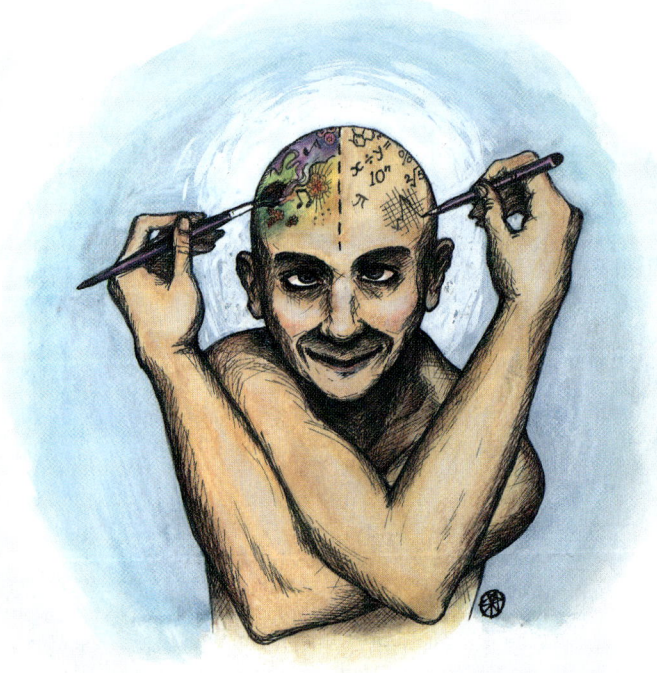

These concepts juxtapose with the concepts of vertical and lateral thinking, proposed and elaborated by DeBono (in COCD, 1999).

Creative thinking requires both **left and right** brain, or convergent and divergent, vertical and lateral thinking (Abra, 1997). Gelb, 1996 calls this **'synvergent'** thinking; to combine convergent (focused, analytic, detailed) and divergent thinking (diffuse, free flowing and imaginative).

'Iron rusts from disuse, stagnant water loses its purity.'

LEONARDO DA VINCI

Is our creative potential related to our **physical condition**? Our brain uses about 30% of the body's oxygen although it is on average about 2.5 % of the body's weight (Gelb, 1996). The influence on creative thinking cannot be denied. 'Vitality of thinking is proportional to health' (McKim, 1980). Just as our attitudes have a profound effect on our body, the body has a profound effect on the mind.

The creative process

Preparation
Incubation
Unconscious incubation
Illumination
Verification
(CLEMEN, 1996)

Preparation
Generation
Incubation phase
Evaluation
Implementation
(GELB, 1996)

Problem description
Briefing: 'The problem as given' ,
Formulation and reformulation
'The problem as understood'

Idea development
Purge
Creative move

Critical step
Clustering
Selection
Criteria check

Final report and action planning
(COCD, 1999)

Find the problem
Find the facts around the problem
Define the problem
Find ideas
Evaluate and select solutions from ideas
Plan actions upon the selections
Gain acceptance for the solutions
Take action on the solutions
(BASADUR SIMPLEX PROBLEM SOLVING PROCESS)
(MARTIN, 1998)

Generative – memory retrieval, association, mental synthesis, mental transformation, analogical transfer, categorical reduction

Exploratory – attribute finding, conceptual interpretation, functional inference, contextual shifting, hypothesis testing, searching for limitations
(GENOPLORE MODEL; FINKE *ET AL*, 1992)

Inspiration
Clarification
Distillation
Perspiration
Evaluation
Incubation
(PETTY, 1997)

Imaginative insight
Find ratios
Rational insight
Imaginative fancy
Rational fancy
(BOHM, 1998)

These proposed creative processes arising from the various approaches in the literature are all very similar and can be generalised as preparation, generation, incubation, verification as follows:

Preparation

In this initial stage the problem or question is defined, reformulated and redefined, moving from a given to an understanding. The way in which the question is formulated severely influences the solution finding ability. Instead of seeking the right answer, one can ask 'Is this the right question?' Gelb, 1996 points out that our move from a nomadic way of life to settlement occurred by reformulating the question, 'How do we get to the water?' to ' How can we make the water come to us?'

Generation

'If you want to get a good idea, get a lot of ideas.'
LINUS PAULLING (2 X NOBEL PRIZE) IN GELB, 1996

This stage involves 'moving beyond habitual pathways of thinking' (Gelb, 1996) by purging associative concepts to the problem. Osborn described generation as brainstorming. Osborn furthermore sets up principles for brainstorming: Quantity breeds quality; Postponement of judgement; Hitch-hiking (building on other peoples' ideas); and Free-wheeling (continuing unrelated fantasy). The purge aims to shake out all ideas, even the most obvious ones, as they may hinder the mind from looking further (Osborn in COCD, 1999).

In this phase a 'creative move' can then be applied. Examples of such moves are described in 'Creative techniques'.

Incubation

'A part of you is much smarter than you are.'
GELB, 1996

As well as being part of most creative developments, incubation can act on its own, as a subconscious stimuli to an inventive concept. Studies have shown that individuals frequently generate a potential idea after a certain time of incubation (sleep, shower, biking, sailing etc), a period of full relaxation or relaxed attention (Tomic and Brouwers, 1998). It allows one's sub-intentional intelligence to suggest solutions. 'Brain researchers estimate that the unconscious database outweighs the conscious on an order exceeding 10 million to one. This database is the source of your hidden natural creative genius' (Gelb, 1996). The great creative thinkers have used this method throughout history. Einstein instructed his students to include incubation as a necessary part of all their cognition; Kekule, the discoverer of the benzene ring, scheduled incubation/daydreaming periods into his daily work programme (Buzan 1999). An unusual assignment has been demonstrated by Goldschmidt (1999):

'I commission every student to dream a solution to a problem they are living through right now. If they are unable to come up with such a dream they have to go to the library and find the biographical records of five people who have solved things through dreams. It's amazing how many of the kids manage to have the dream by the time they are down to the second or third biography search.'

'I call intuition cosmic fishing, you feel a nibble then you've got to hook the fish, after baiting the hook through preparation and generation, and trolling deep waters with incubation, it's time to reel in the catch' (Buckminster Fuller in Gelb, 1996).

Verification

After incubation the new links are purged, all the ideas are analysed, clustered and evaluated, (COCD, 1999) followed by planning the action and implementation.

Creativity techniques

Many techniques have been proposed for developing creativity. In most cases these have been experientially developed and tested. They are not based on cognitive models, although it is often suggested that they may be improved once cognitive studies are in a position to be able to develop their own input. Techniques are often 'creative moves' situated in the generation phase, after the purge, as described previously. Several techniques, however, are fully elaborated as complete processes.

The basic technique in creativity is to increase the possible alternatives, which mostly happens during the generation phase. A basic creative move involves listing the assumptions regarding the problem or question, breaking through each assumption by asking 'What if this weren't true?' and reviewing the problem (COCD, 1999). It is not within the scope of this book to provide a 'toolkit' for creativity techniques so only two examples of the very different techniques are presented in detail below. Further examples are:

Analogy with nature or biomimetics (Baillie, 1999)

Analogy: provocative, paradoxical, personal (COCD, 1999)

Metaphorical thinking (Clemen, 1996)

Brain writing (Rohrbach in COCD, 1999)

Dynamic brain writing (Rohrbach, in COCD, 1999)

MATEC (Créarggie, in COCD, 1999)

Synectics (William Gordon, in Martin 1998)

TRIZ

Mind mapping (Buzan, 1999)

Storyboarding (Disney in Martin, 1998)

Role play (Gelb, 1996; COCD, 1999)

TRIZ

'Always, but not always with...'

Probably the strongest creativity technique is called TRIZ, the Theory of Inventive Problem Solving. TRIZ began with the analysis of 2.5 million patents and has been developed by over 1500 man-years of research. The key findings of TRIZ research are:

1. All innovations emerge from only 40 inventive principles
2. Technological trends are highly predictable
3. The strongest solutions transform unwanted or harmful elements into useful resources
4. The strongest solutions overcome the conflicts of trade-offs, upon which most design practice is based

The basic process for creating good solutions is based upon the practice of mapping specific problems to a generic problem which has already been solved elsewhere. In this short section a number of the fundamentals will be introduced behind both TRIZ as a philosophy and its most useful tools.

Philosophy

The first pillar of TRIZ is the notion of IDEALITY – always increasing the benefits whilst eliminating both cost and harm. This perspective allows you to work backwards from the ideal solution to a solution achievable now. An ideal solution requires minimal addition and optimal use of RESOURCES. Indeed the idea of maximizing use of available resources is fundamental, for example the use of saliva to stick stamps or the use of readily available nitrogen gas to protect crisps in packets both chemically and physically.

The second pillar of TRIZ is the concept of FUNCTIONALITY, identifying the purpose and effects of each element in a system. Any effect that does not help perform the function is ultimately harmful or wasteful. In addition, once the function has been identified it is possible to find other methods to perform the function i.e. *'Solutions change, functions stay the same'*. Having mapped a specific function to a generic function, solutions can be found using a 'KNOWLEDGE DATABASE' that draws on prior knowledge and experience from all fields. For the function r*emoving water*, once mapped to the generic function *move liquid*, the knowledge database can provide 33 methods for moving 'your' water.

TRIZ tools

The idea of a contradiction is fundamental to the use of TRIZ. Traditionally, most common solutions accept trade-offs. A table for example, encounters the trade-off between strength and weight. These have been collated in the CONTRADICTION MATRIX, where a comparison of the factors in the contradiction suggests a number of inventive principles that have previously been used to solve it. The contradiction matrix suggests that the typical trade-off for a table can be avoided with the use of composite materials or dividing it into parts. Knowledge classification by function allows direct access to the alternative methods.

Possibly the most interesting finding was the predictability of technological change. As such, 35 TRENDS OF EVOLUTION have been identified that allow the development of a solution to be predicted. Below a number of examples illustrate the successive application of the trend to increase mobility (dynamisation):

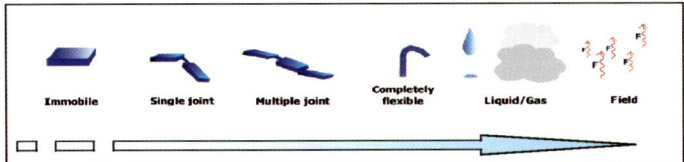

These products were developed over a long period of time however TRIZ uses the knowledge gained from studying other fields and products to predict these steps in advance.

In short

The philosophical aspects combined with the tools make TRIZ not only an aid to creativity but also a guide for that creativity based on prior knowledge, thus increasing the efficiency of the process and the likelihood of finding a stronger solution. Additionally, the principles and ideas within TRIZ have proven to be both applicable and effective across all domains. Its depth and versatility enable it to be adapted to any individual, further increasing its popularity.

For more information see: www.TRIZ.info

Analogy with nature – biomimetics

Increasingly researchers in engineering are becoming aware of the power of learning from nature. Mimicking nature is not new, of course, as we have been inspired by nature for many centuries – did we think of making nets before observing spiders' webs? Was velcro invented before or after observing burrs?

This approach can be transferred to any problem which needs to be solved. In the generation phase of creativity, ideas can be further explored and thoughts developed by looking at them from a completely different direction. Questions may be posed such as 'How would nature solve this problem?' 'What have you seen in nature which reminds you of this?' The problem may need to be redefined several times. In fact, researchers who use this approach take several different paths: exact analogy – copying what nature does to solve the problem as set, eg. velcro; principle analogy – using ideas from nature's ways of solving one problem and applying them to a different setting. For example, when developing tough coatings for impact resistance by studying shells, the exact structure is not copied but certain principles are learnt about how to improve toughness; and idea generation – natural objects, materials and processes are studied and ideas emerge which might have varied applications, an example of problem finding.

Team based problem solving for engineers

PAUL WALKER, CAROLINE BAILLIE AND SIMON DEWULF

The case:
Master of Research students
PhD students
University College London
The research:
Observation
Filming active sessions
Focus group – videoed students
Email feedback students

Creativity guidelines
Personal development
Intrigue
Humour
Convergent and Divergent thinking
Handing over responsibility
Environment
Intensive one week course

Introduction

The course observed in this case study was an off-campus four-day introduction to a skills development programme for research students at UCL, most of them on a one-year MRes (Master of Research) course, some working for a PhD, mostly in their first year. The programme, Personal and Professional Skills in Research Practice (PPSRP) is an integral part of the MRes programme at UCL, providing 20% of the assessment for the degree, which can be awarded at Pass or Distinction level. The PPSRP module takes students from a variety of disciplinary groups across science and engineering and brings them together for one full week early in the academic year, and thereafter every Friday for two terms.

The range of learning/teaching methods used over the full programme includes traditional lecturing, workshop-style tutorials, simulation games involving teamwork and creative problem solving, reflective articulation, agenda setting, critical reviews of case study material, presentation of findings and reflective review of their experience of learning in different disciplinary contexts, including working on major research projects. All these were present to some degree in the off-campus course at Cwm Pennant, which could be seen as a stand-alone programme taking a first cut at issues developed in more detail during the remainder of the course.

Creating oneself

Students took part in discussion and reflection before and during the off-campus course regarding particular skills they would target for development in the programme. This agenda-setting was an important foundation for the course and the creativity to be encouraged within it. Having students in the role of passive recipients in a pre-scripted process is a strong disincentive for the expression of creativity and a deep approach to learning. A view of a deep approach to learning expressed in higher education research literature is of a process in which the learner 'changes as a person'. This is considered to be particularly relevant to skills development programmes. It is also possible to take a deeper cut and suggest that the ultimate expression of creativity is where one 'creates oneself', both in self-perception and in forming developmental intention.

Creativity in groups

The students knew beforehand that they would be working sometimes in small teams (10 of six or seven members), at other times in larger groups (two of ~30 members, referred to during the course as 'companies') and that the structuring of these groups would be largely under their own management. Also the structuring of their activities would be handed over to them progressively during the four days of the course. This, too, was considered to be relevant to creativity – not only do the tasks themselves require creativity, but the students would be creating the infrastructure to support the design and execution of those tasks. While 'creating oneself' is a somewhat subliminal and elusive process, creating a team or company as an extension of oneself is more accessible and available for explicit examination.

Process versus product

The first task assigned was intended to turn what would otherwise be a mundane necessity into a challenge, aiming for high performance and creation of the organisational infrastructure to achieve the goals. Since at least some of the first two days would be spent outdoors, the students required packed lunches. If each person were to make and pack his or her own lunch, the process could probably be achieved in a reasonable time with an acceptable result.

However, it was decided to set the task as an organisational production process, with each company required to make a set of lunches to specification, with a notified number of vegetarian lunches to be provided. A feedback form was also to be packed in each lunch. Lunches were to be made within a 20-minute time limit after breakfast and the entire process was to occur within a marked area, the safety and hygiene of which was the responsibility of the company. Each company had to appoint a production manager, to whom the specifications were provided the evening before and who would be responsible for organising the production process in which each company member was expected to play a role.

The two companies were competing and assessed on a number of criteria (such as health & safety, quality of product, environmental management, utilisation of resources, etc). Video recordings and observers' notes were taken during the execution phase of the process and used as a basis for review and improvement for the second day. When each set of lunches was produced, the companies were informed that they had just produced a product for the other company (which came as a surprise) and the sets of lunches were duly swapped.

This was repeated on the second day, when improvements apparent from the self-review of the process and the feedback from customers, were implemented. The first day was, predictably, chaotic with the result being marginally achieved – customer feedback was on the whole quite negative. It was thus particularly interesting that, rather than the companies taking a simply remedial approach and implementing improvements to bring the current process up to standard, they each spontaneously increased the specifications – in particular they took individual orders from customers in advance rather than supplying a standard set lunch as previously. They succeeded in meeting the higher product specifications, using a visibly more efficient process, with a greater level of involvement and enthusiasm from all company members.

Lightheartedness

This process is described in detail as an example of the success of a particular design rationale for the course, and one which underpins the fostering of creativity. By setting the scene to call forth extraordinary, rather than reasonable, performance and leaving the means of accomplishing the task sufficiently open within well-defined boundaries, creative thinking was called for. It is essential that this be set up in a way that encourages enthusiasm in a somewhat lighthearted atmosphere. Creativity can be diminished rather than fostered if the process becomes too earnest. The difference in quality of participation and outcome between the first and second days of this process attests to the success of this endeavour.

Convergent and divergent thinking

The first day of the course was devoted to both outdoor simulation games promoting creative problem-solving in small teams and to classroom reflections on personal and general issues concerning skill development. It must be stressed that the experiential games (which altogether occupied about a quarter of the course) were reviewed by the participants and staff in a way in which relevance to academic and professional experience was brought to the fore in a convergent manner, which allowed for divergent thinking. In the sandwich production exercise outlined above, the relevance to communication, negotiation, task assignment and management was developed in review sessions on the first and second days.

The other two experiential games on the course also had their relevance highlighted, but in the interests of developing creativity and lighthearted enthusiasm, an additional element of imaginative fantasy scenarios was designed. The centre's outdoor circuit of physical problem-solving tasks became part of an imaginative story line that connected them in an epic escape from hostile pursuers. The tongue-in-cheek tone of the briefings was in part designed to set the mood of somewhat 'off-the-wall' participation, again as a stimulus to creativity.

The environment

The fictional scenario within the off-campus scenario was regarded by many students, as well as the course designers, as an important aspect of skills development. Several students have remarked during feedback that in that environment they were willing to try new approaches, not consistent with their familiar self-image. The effect of the environment in stimulating creativity was marked both in the creative solving of externalised problems, including organisational problems arising, and in the creation 'within' of unfamiliar attitudes and behaviours.

It was the experience of solving these problems and intentionally going beyond the boundaries of the familiar that was the focus of the classroom sessions occupying the other half of the first day and on other days. One particular issue which drew attention was the nature of excellence, both individually and collectively – what was required to produce extraordinary performance and excellence systematically rather than by a judgement in hindsight of who might have won the race?

Handing over responsibility

The second day was also a mixture of classroom sessions and a simulation game within an imaginary scenario. The difference was that the game was conducted in competition between the companies, with the organisation of smaller teams within the companies being handed over to the students themselves. This handing over of responsibility was intended to offer the opportunity for creativity as well, and both groups appeared to seize that opportunity enthusiastically, making several organisational and technical mistakes in the process, but correcting them (with some angst) and ultimately reaching a successful conclusion, with consequent spirited celebrations.

Even greater creativity was exhibited by the half-dozen facilitators, all of whom had taken part in some training in facilitation techniques beforehand. The team of facilitators wrote company briefings, acting the parts as required, including an assessment of the company infrastructure set up in response to briefing criteria. They also set the clues and tasks which together formed the progressively developing solution of a somewhat cloak-and-dagger mystery set in the environs of the centre.

The overall solution required technical skills as well as lateral thinking and coordinated teamwork. The intensive burst of creativity among the facilitators working under extreme pressure was remarkable, and a further illustration of the suggested correlation between carefully managed pressure for extraordinary performance, enthusiasm, a twist of the bizarre and creativity.

Taking the creative ideas forward

On the final two days of the course, the responsibility for task and company organisation was further handed over to the students, with a much more open brief for innovative product design and development being presented to the companies.

The product to be designed and presented as a proposal to an evaluation panel was a skills development exercise or sub-programme suitable for the site and/or environs. This assignment is set up as an analogue to research and development proposals which would be submitted in a competitive bidding process. These would be ranked by a panel composed of a variety of interested parties, with successful bids being funded or in some way progressing to a further stage.

The choice of a skills development exercise or sub-programme as a matter for proposal and design was for both feasibility within the timescale and as a deepening of the learning arising from previous experiences, in which the students' role was more passive.

In the classroom sessions that were interspersed through the four days of the course, the students took a very active role in articulating the learning points and capturing these in written summary form. Some of this process has been captured on videotape, and a booklet was produced from these summaries and distributed among the participating students.

Evaluation

The course was designed not only to foster creativity, but to achieve a multiplicity of objectives. It may be the synergistic interaction between these various developmental themes that enhanced the individual aspects. Students were still referring back to events in this off-campus course several months later, and requested a follow-up event be organised toward the end of the academic year, subscribed on a voluntary basis at their own expense. More than half of the MRes

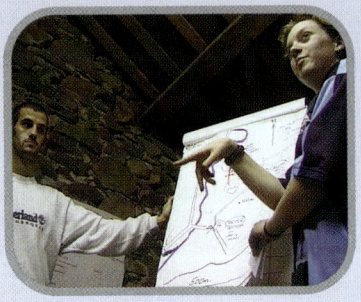

students signed up for this course, and approximately three-quarters of them applied for training as facilitators for other courses.

A major issue in the ultimate effectiveness of courses of this kind is the extent to which the creative spirit evident in the immediate course environment is transferred to the normal environment.

A focus group interview conducted some months after the initial course indicated that many students were actively reflecting on the ways they normally went about doing things, and that they now saw things differently, with a much more open framework of interpretation. They referred to several ways in which they had cooperatively created ways of interacting with each other and their departmental systems, some of which were very successful.

Others appeared to conflict with their departmental tutors' expectations and were discouraged. The expression of creativity in a familiar environment, especially when the cultural expectations are strong but implicit, was problematic for many of the individuals whose creativity had been stimulated in a short-term extra-mural event like this.

A course like this is evidently highly beneficial but takes a great deal of careful design beforehand and skilful management during the event. This is time-consuming, and in effect adds to the expense of the course, which is high when travel and accommodation costs are taken into account. While this kind of course can run against the grain of normal academic culture, its concentration into a few days makes it easier for postgraduate research students to participate.

Creativity Guidelines

Personal development – ability to develop personal awareness
Intrigue – sense of intrigue and excitement of discovery
Humour – every exercise performed with a sense of fun
Convergent and divergent thinking – seeing the relevance and focusing on the value and learning potential of the exercises
Handing over responsibility gradually during the week
Environment, outdoors, free from normal constraint
Intensive one week course

Encouraging innovation in graduate engineers

BAS SAJIK, CAROLINE BAILLIE AND SIMON DEWULF

The case:
BOC Gases
Graduate engineers
The research:
Observations
Presentation by group facilitator
Filming active sessions
Focus group discussion graduates
Facilitator feedback
Discussion with Innovation Director

Creativity guidelines
Idea template
Company wide access
White think group
Young people
Rewards as well as satisfactions
Director of innovation
Interdisciplinarity
Matching creativity with experience

Introduction

The BOC Group began trading in 1886 as the Brin's Oxygen Company. A technology to extract oxygen from the air had just been developed and the Brin brothers started production at a factory in Westminster, London. Growth came from finding new uses for these gases, new customers, and new markets.

Today BOC Gases focuses on eight global market sectors: electronics, chemicals and petroleum, food, glass, metals, minerals, fabrication and medical; and is encouraging product and process innovation worldwide. New products include a new synthetic liquefied air product, an ozone-based wastewater treatment, a process for recovery and recycling of hydrocarbon emissions and so on.

Creativity versus innovation

This case needed to address the difference between creativity and innovation. As a working definition creativity can be looked upon as 'shared imagination'. Once a creative idea finds a route for commercialisation, ie. an application within a market, it becomes an innovation. If the creative idea is not domain-specific it becomes an invention.

For a creative idea to become an innovation, it needs entrepreneurs to support and market the idea along the innovation path, foreseeing complementarity in current company production. In most industries this challenge is imperfectly solved and idea development is hindered by inefficiencies and high transaction costs. BOC Gases has formulated an 'idea template' and a 'white think group' to facilitate the innovation process.

29

The idea template

'Every idea should be recorded, we are not the people to judge.'

INNOVATION DIRECTOR, BOC

Innovation promoters often encourage the use of a 'creation database', but it is considered by BOC that the development of ideas in this way often lacks direction. The aspect of ownership and end-point are not well defined, neither is the way to get there .

At BOC any staff member is encouraged to submit ideas through an idea template, a set of questions which defines all aspects of the idea. The idea template allows creative people from all over the company to input, and take ownership for, their new concepts within a standardised entry format and leads them through different steps of the creation process. Promising ideas are taken forward for discussion within the white think group, so that the richness of the creation increases through the blending of the competencies.

The Idea Template

1.0 Product Definition

1.1 Product Title
Short working Name

1.2 Idea Management
Whose original idea was it?
Who is managing the idea?

1.3 Product Definition
Long-term objective of the product development

1.4 Market Definition
Target markets & dimensions incl. internal customers

1.5 Customer Benefits
What difference would this make to our customers

2.0 Commercialisation

2.1 Business Alignment
Is this step new, or does it complement existing problems?

2.2 Business Strategy
Brief description of how this product could be marketed and by whom

2.3 Technical Strategy
What technology must be developed? How and by whom?

3.0 Contingency Planning

3.1 Competition & IPR
Who are the competitors?
What are they doing?
How do we keep ahead?

3.2 Contingencies
What could go wrong?
How could we get around them?

3.3 Product Definition
What will stop the project proceeding any further?

4.0 Rough Cost-Benefit Analysis
4.1 BOC Prize
Estimate the commercial value of opportunity to BOC

4.2 Probability of success
Based on risks and show stoppers

4.3 Cost to Commercialisation
Estimate total cost to develop and launch

4.4 Go/No-Go?
Should this be proposed for a Gate 0 Review? If no, can it be Improved?

5.0 Other Supporting Information

The white think group

At BOC Gases a **'white think group'** (WTG) was formed for promoting new ideas and developing them through focused discussion into proposals for innovative products. The WTG is predominantly drawn from those on the BOC Graduate schemes (three to five years), or those who have recently left. They bring fresh approaches and gain confidence in the field.

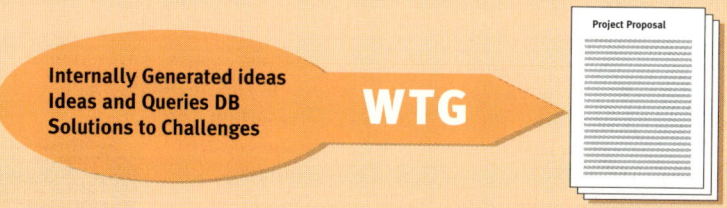

Within the different departments of BOC there are white spaces in which WTG is looking for ideas and innovations that can be developed to a new process or product.

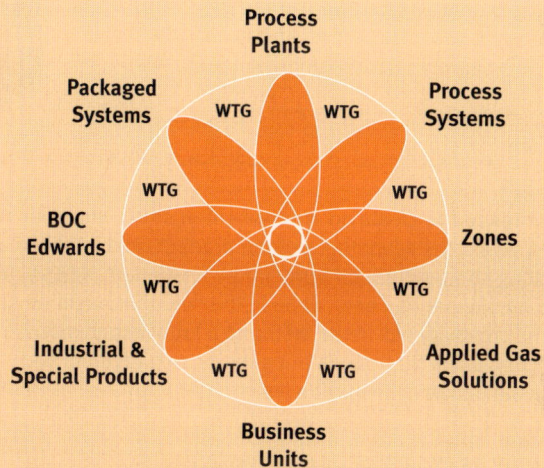

The WTG, often comprised of innovators themselves, is asked to take ideas further. They may also be called on to brainstorm ideas for solutions to existing problems. Once the ideas are well defined (through the template and WTG), a report is completed to pass **Gate Zero** to see whether it is worth pursuing the idea.

The project proposal will then be discussed with the Innovation Director and relevant specialists. The project is finally presented to a suitable gate-keeping audience.

Exploring ideas in group sessions

Examples of two ideas, typically drawn out by WTG, are given below:

'I have a dream... sleeping gas proposal.'

The 'sleeping gas' product can be defined as a small inhaler device to deliver gas, which has a soporific effect, similar to the concept of an asthma inhaler or an air freshener dispenser. It is a safer/ easier alternative to sleeping tablets. The markets can be defined as consumer and domestic, as well as hospitals. The business/ alignment strategy could then be 'safer, adjustable dosage, more accessible and less daunting. Thus the idea finds its structure in the idea template and is now ready for discussion by the WTG. The questions raised within the group are: 'What drug can we use for it? Is it soluble? Can we use the device for other drugs? What is the time to knockout? What has already been done (using a patent search)? Heart safety? What are the showstoppers?'

'Domestic aroma gas'

This is a product intended to create an atmosphere or smell, energetic or calming in different locations. Again the advantages of the product can be looked at in the context of its existing competitors: oil-burners, air fresheners, and so on. Here it was discovered that a lot of work had been done in the field that might be applied to this particular idea. The creativity lies in the WTG and a lot of experience is present elsewhere in the company. The group is bringing the two together with the catalyst of the process being the ability to see problems.

'Problem makers are as important as creative thinkers.'

Encouraging different perspectives

A group of up to about 10 people is the maximum for productive communication, giving everyone the chance to listen and speak. There is no hierarchical setup of the group and judgement is postponed, putting down all ideas on a clipboard. The group members role-play to evaluate the challenges and opportunities of the idea presented. During the meeting, the angle of approach has been stimulated by different attitudes towards the problem, for example, 'what if...?' or 'what are showstoppers?'. The process is similar to the 'six thinking hats' elaborated by DeBono, where each team member must approach the problem from his/her hat's perspective. This technique is used by several companies including Rolls-Royce when training graduates:

White hat: Information and data

Green hat: Creativity, alternatives and new ideas

Black hat: Caution, risks and difficulties

Yellow hat: Benefits and useable concepts

Red hat: Feelings and emotions

Blue hat: Managing the thinking and process control

Applying this technique results in more productive meetings and gives space for creative thinking. It also encourages 'parallel thinking', reduces conflict, improves teamwork, encourages contribution and results in better decisions.

'Hopefully new ideas will make or save money, and also help to develop new skills.'

Creativity guidelines

- It allows anyone within the company with an idea to submit it.
- The company benefits from a wide range of technology. The ability to create new ideas depends largely upon the knowledge of individuals in different fields.
- Young people are allowed to develop their creative potential. The WTG has not adapted to a generic 'company blindness' way of thinking. They come to the company with very different backgrounds and very diverse opinions. They are in the position of being creative as well as relying on the company's experience to guide their proposals.
- High ranking rewards as well as the satisfaction of witnessing a personal idea through different stages of development, (I have a dream was the title of the sleeping gas project). The several stages to completion become familiar to the idea owner. Every stage opens new perspectives and can trigger off very different markets for the original idea, for example the sleeping gas device can contain a range of different drugs.
- The existence of an Innovation Director to support creativity within the company.
- Interdisciplinarity within the company and the creation of ideas between the various disciplines (white space).
- The template has shown its vital contribution to the creation of new ideas.

Creative materials engineering: polymers

CAROLINE BAILLIE AND SIMON DEWULF

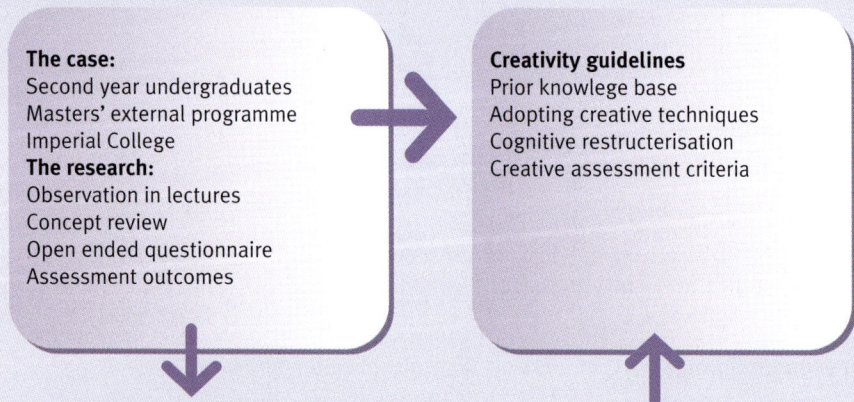

The case:
Second year undergraduates
Masters' external programme
Imperial College
The research:
Observation in lectures
Concept review
Open ended questionnaire
Assessment outcomes

Creativity guidelines
Prior knowlege base
Adopting creative techniques
Cognitive restructerisation
Creative assessment criteria

Interactive teaching – creating understanding

In 1996 a new approach was introduced to a polymer science core course within a Materials Science degree at Imperial College. A text was produced for the course notes, which was used as a basis for discussion, instead of traditional lectures, to encourage more active learning. Activities ranged from role-plays, poster sessions, small group discussions, quizzes, debates, case studies and problem classes, to demonstrations of experiments by researchers.

Some lecturing was retained to reduce student anxiety over 'new' methods. In the debates they were to think about the use of models for understanding mechanical properties, they had to make a decision about whether modelling helped or oversimplified. In the role-plays they had to 'become' a polymer chain. What did it feel like to be viscoelastic? In the classic 'creative move' students were asked to think 'outside the box' and find an analogy or redefine the problem, moving from the rational to the imaginary and back again. Students in this context were creating their own understanding.

The exam was fairly tightly prescribed but it was possible to develop a four part question which looked traditional but in fact used a learning hierarchy.

Interactive creation

- Students were asked to create knowledge about the next step. Rather than the lecturer producing an overhead with a series of concepts, the students were asked to be involved in the process of linking development and building understanding. This took a lot of preparation and required the lectures to be given in a particular order. Use of analogy or demonstrations may be needed to aid this conceptual development.

- When facing a problem of molecular understanding students were asked to imagine through their natural behaviour what the small-scaled sequence of events might be. Their experience of the system settings was often enough to predict the outcome of the situation. In searching for the required properties of an application material, descriptions often started off lyrically then converged into hard science. Again students were able to structure their personal opinions and perceptions into a communicative plan of action.

- Emphasis on active learning, proactive creation of knowledge. The idea builds on ongoing research into knowledge building which suggests that for optimum creative thinking, seeing things from a variety of perspectives other than one's own was essential. Hence opinions were encouraged and the use of techniques such as line-ups, where the class placed themselves on a line according to their belief about a particular issue.

We discussed the problem given in conjunction with our notes. Talking to people gives you new ideas and ways of thinking

STUDENTS

Curriculum content

This was altered by:

 i) some obsolete, old fashioned and unnecessary parts being removed;

 ii) an additional session of biomimetics, recycling and the future of polymers;

iii) content being reorganised so that all parts linked and made sense, by using students' prior knowledge and their day to day observations as a base.

The course then became a series of questions to be answered:

- **Classification** – what is it?
- **Processing** – how is it made?
- **Structure** – What does it look like? What does that mean?
- **Properties** – How does it behave?
- **Characterisation** – How do you know what it is?
- **The future** – What effect will polymers have on our future?
- **Mechanical behaviour** – How can we test polymers? Why is a polymer stiff when cold and ductile when hot?

Knowledge base

The students related to a knowledge base with which they were familiar to provide a safe environment for creative thinking. The first session was understandably difficult in terms of getting the students used to participation in lectures. This was done by throwing bottles of shampoo and cleansing gel around the room, guessing how each was made and thus the identity of its polymer.

Brainstorming

Brainstorming was introduced at the beginning of the class to bring the students' knowledge base to the forefront and to ease the flow of ideas, helping them feel comfortable with the idea of speaking aloud. At the start of every session, students brainstormed by coming up with as many associations as possible for a given subject. Unsurprisingly most of the subjects to be discussed were articulated during the brainstorming. Individual students became the problem-owner of the subject and therefore experienced personal involvement. From the brainstorming sessions, the lecturer was able to cluster subjects into the units of the course.

The brainstorming sessions were well accepted and by the third lecture, the students needed no prompting to call out their ideas. The restructured material was far easier to teach because of its logical concept development. Each point led onto another, rather than being a seemingly unrelated series of facts. This made it easier for the students to develop their own understanding. Also in the third lecture, the students were asked to predict from their new found manner of thinking and brainstorming ideas, the results of some research experiments and the implications for material properties. Some responses were creative indeed, even promoting ideas to be followed up by PhD students. Feedback from the students suggested they realised the importance of the brainstorming sessions. Some responses are as follows:

(They) activate the mind
Get people to think for themselves and develop ideas from scratch
(Are) a way of introducing the main ideas covered in each lecture

STUDENTS

Brainstorming also allowed the lecturer to measure students' prior knowledge on a given subject. The students themselves were able to face their prior knowledge and experience the value of their own reasoning. This was absolutely vital if the new information was to be sustained. Incorrect preconceptions could then be overwritten with 'new' concepts.

Creative assessment

Most of the above involves creative thinking and not too much creativity in the sense of developing an idea into a product. The most productive creative session involved students collecting all the data together from a lab class they had designed themselves from which they chose the best polymer to make a new range of ski goods. They then had to create class strength diagrams for each polymer. The most creative assessment task was the 'user guide' for polymers. They did this as a class and their contributions were bound together to make the '1999 User Guide for Polymer Selection'. It is hoped that this will be useful to the students in their future careers as well as helping to develop their knowledge and skills relating to polymers and presentation.

The exam questions were designed to test the students' ability to think in, what was for them, a very different way. In the first year of the course the exam results were not excellent probably because the students did not have enough time to think creatively in the short period allocated. Indeed students reported informally after the exam that the questions required them to 'think too much.' This highlighted an important problem of assessing this kind of thinking where the lecturer has little control over assessment design.

Student feedback

Feedback via open ended questionnaires indicated that students could see the value of interactive learning and brainstorming (see the italicised comments above). However standard evaluation forms which asked students to give scores out of five for categories such as audibility, timings and clarity of presentation were not appropriate for the course, despite being the official feedback mechanism. Students were not able to understand how to apply the questions to the new style of course, and those who were nervous about the approach gave a uniformly poor score for every category, however meaningless.

Running the course intensively

The polymer course runs very differently as a Masters level external programme in Cairo. Instead of running over a whole term, the course was run intensively, with lecturers taking a course week by week. Hence the 16 hours were run consecutively in small groups, allowing more space for classwork and coffee breaks together. Students were much more motivated – they were graduate engineers and interacted throughout, even during lectures. An attempt was made to present the course in a relevant way to Egyptians by using data from a local recycling plant and solving real problems for the case studies.

Evaluation of the course in its first year was by focus group, which was videoed for analysis. Students discussed freely their reasons for taking the degree, the differences they noticed between this and other courses and its relevance to their careers. Generally the students felt that the polymer course was very different and therefore very challenging, but extremely useful and relevant. They agreed that they would have liked more time to study polymers compared with other materials, despite the fact that all were metallurgists. They also discussed the way they were asked to think and learn.

A comment from one student during a problem class summed up the tone of this discussion:

"So you're testing our thinking? I think I know what you are doing, it's a completely different way of thinking, different for Egypt but also different for London. You are squeezing our brains. You can see it – they're sitting in the front row leaning forward to catch everything you say."

Students on this course did very well in the exams, which were similar in style to the undergraduate course. The ability of the students to see the importance of the interactive style was necessary for the ultimate success of the method. In the Cairo situation this was facilitated by the maturity and professionalism of the students. In an undergraduate setting this would be the biggest challenge, especially if the rest of the degree course remained traditional.

Creativity guidelines

- Make students comfortable so they are at ease, allowing creativity
    - i) Use everyday objects and relate to real life
    - ii) Start from their knowledge base
    - iii) Brainstorm at the start of each lecture with all relevant rules eg. don t mock others and accept everything first time round
- Use of techniques where possible
    - i) Brainstorming sessions
    - ii) Open ended questions
    - iii) Encouragement of diversity
    - iv) Use of analogy
- Emphasis on creation of knowledge from concepts
    - i) Needs conceptual restructuring of content
    - ii) Lecturer to think out the basic concepts
    - iii) Lecturer to be self reflective on how they learn concepts
    - iv) Understand the importance of variation   seeing things from a different perspective, use of line-ups etc
- Rearranging assessment tasks so that the creative thinking' category in departmental guidelines is properly addressed. This is within a categorisation where original thinking and new perspectives are rewarded.

Product development and creative design

CHRIS ROSE, CAROLINE BAILLIE AND SIMON DEWULF

The case:
BA (Hons) Three-dimensional Crafts
BA (Hons) 3D Design for Production ,
University of Brighton

The research:
Interviews with members of staff,
third-year students (quotes in italic)
Observations at the Brighton site
Discussions of the outcomes

Creativity guidelines:
Foundation year
Visual research
Switching convergent-divergent
thinking –
Incubation
Assessment – critique (group-peer)
Personal approach
Building confidence through
self-awareness
Working within barriers
Open briefings – divergent problems

Foundation year (prior to Brighton degree course)

'You have to loosen up, to show what's inside of you. Do something, which is part of you. It is coming from the inside, which touches you...'

STUDENT

Prior to the University degree, applicants take a foundation year. The aim of this year is to set aside the GCSE/A level curriculum approach, to look at what is possible, what the individuals' real strengths, weaknesses and preferences are and to identify the appropriate degree route for further development of the individual's talents. A mixture of set projects or topics followed by a personal or self-directed project are studied and students are given tutorial guidance both in groups and one to one. Critique involves staff and students in groups where both content and execution are expounded, criticised and developed.

Contact teaching varies considerably according to which course/college is involved. This year permits students to experience the aims of the courses, and they are given the opportunity to try out different fields and different materials. It permits individuals to loosen up from their restrictive backgrounds, and develop their personal approach to the course. The foundation year is experienced as exciting as the individual becomes open to a sea of possibilities, challenges and fields in which he or she can create a personal curriculum.

The degree course

Teaching is a mixture of lectures/seminars/one to one discussion of project development/group reviews and formal critiques/assessments where students' ability to select and present their best work is important. Student work is carried out in workshops with the support of specialist technicians and academic staff. All student work is self initiated during the latter half of the three year degree.

Idea development

During the initial stage of the degree course, students are given a briefing of concepts to research and create, supported by incremental technical demonstration and information. It is then open for interpretation to create an item of personal context, within the given parameters. The student interprets the challenge, conducts visual research and experiments with ideas. By means of drawing, collage, photography, model making and tests with materials, the visual research brings together elements from different fields directly or indirectly related to the idea, giving the student a wide range of idea generation. Visual research is a significant step in the idea development and will be discussed in greater detail below.

At the initial stages of development students diverge their thinking, giving their minds free associative flow which is expressed in their visual research work. The briefing also initiates an incubation period, in which students subconsciously immerse themselves into the subject.

Once appropriate materials are selected, new boundaries become apparent, giving direction to further development of the concept. If problems appear, one can always go back to the initial ideas illustrated within the visual research. The final stage becomes a linear process in producing the concept. This is where the student switches from a divergent dominated process to a more convergent production process. An assessment panel assesses the final outcome, making the critique part of the learning process. Students are often very critical of their own productions. The feelings expressed seem to be a balance of seeing the 'opportunity for improvement' (the majority describe themselves as perfectionist) and decisions taken to proceed.

In parallel with individual research, students are taught technical skills in a variety of material processes, through demonstration and application to individual ideas.

Visual research

'It is a course that makes you look at other things, the more you look, the more you want to do.'
STUDENT

The more you know, the more you can know and the more you know there is to know. Visual research becomes an extensive exploration of the given subject. In their visual research students represent fractions of ideas in three dimensional shapes, pictures of related objects, drawings of possible outcomes, and so on. This acts as an advanced purge or brainstorming where words are replaced by pictures, drawings and objects associated with primary divergent thinking. The composition also acts as an idea logbook for personal reference and where anyone can view the development steps taken during the process of creation. It is also possible to gain impressions of possible solutions or results, without being hampered by an over-specific finished product.

As an instrument of investigation and discovery, visual research aims to encourage the 'finding' of personal imagery. This is achieved by providing a wide experience of both two- and three-dimensional techniques and by involving the students in experiences engendering curiosity and enthusiasm for all the diverse practices which may precede the making of three-dimensional artefacts. Visual research includes analytical study, life drawing, model making, conceptual and imaginative studies, technical drawing and colour studies.

Material

' It all works hand in hand, without the materials, the ideas don't move forward.'

STUDENT

Working within the limitations of a given material becomes a challenge. Before starting with the actual material, the object is conceptualised within the student's mind. Working as a three-dimensional thinking vehicle, the visual imagination then needs to be translated onto paper and into maquettes for it to be communicated both to the student and to tutors.

Technicians are available for technical support in specialist areas – wood, metal, ceramics, plastics, photography, for example. Academic staff and visiting tutors (who are practising artists, craftspeople and product designers) provide tutorial support both in terms of detailed development (eg. 'how can I achieve this concept using vacuum-formed elements?') and general, contextual support and critical references. Academic support is also concerned with encouraging a strategic approach to developing confidence for the individual student.

An example of this might concern advice on how to further develop a wood furniture concept using renewable timber, how to reference this and find sources of information and advice that may lie outside the course.

Some students prefer more straightforward technical support in the earlier stages but appear to appreciate the broader type of mixed technical and contextual support from academic tutors and practitioners later on.

Divergent – convergent thinking

'...if engineers could throw themselves into problems and environments which are alien to them, taking them completely out of the context of being engineer... into a situation where they are really required to use their own imagination in a very rapid way...'

STUDENT

During the development of the idea, students predominantly think divergently and convergently at different times. Divergent thinking is diffuse, free flowing and imaginative. Convergent thinking is focused, analytical and detailed. They start off with a very associative, imaginative open approach to the problem setting. Towards completion students converge their efforts into the final outcome. Thinking as a whole becomes ambidextrous.

Incubation

'I leave it for four months, I am then subconsciously working.'

STUDENT

Students describe idea impulses after sleep, everyday life, periods of relaxed attention etc. In the incubation phase one's sub-attentional mind sorts through all the data collected, all the possibilities played with in the generation phase and puts them all together.

Assessment – critique

The critique is a presentation of what has been done in relation to the student's stated intentions. A statement of intent precedes the three-dimensional work and is used as a basis for tutorial support in the development of projects. A group of around eight to ten students plus a staff member will exchange reactions, critical views and insights around each other's work – either 'work in progress' or at a finished stage.

The majority of the course is intended to be diagnostic for the student ie. testing out the match between intention, skills, ideas and results. A failure to conclude a particular project may still have been a constructive learning experience in the larger programme, providing the student has reflected upon it and taken a different approach subsequently. Students fill in self-assessment project sheets which are then contributed to by staff. In group critiques, the tutor can take the opportunity to refer emerging concepts or issues to a larger audience, giving some perspective on how to make progress towards a stated objective.

Students form clearly visualised goals and get accurate feedback on their current performance. Both are essential to the creative process. Clear vision without accurate feedback will lead to delusion and dreaming in a fantasy world. Accurate feedback without vision misses inspiration and becomes stagnant. Students create clear conscious creative visualisations and seek accurate feedback.

'You can separate the strength of a concept from the strength of the execution.'

TUTOR

From the assessor's perspective, although students' work comes from different angles, they produce very measurable outcomes within which it is possible to see the potential of a concept. The work can be assessed on the basis of that achievement, whether the concept was strong or weak and the realisation was strong or weak.

'I assess my work all the time, find imperfections, change it, push it further into perfection.'

STUDENT

Students assess their work during the whole process. Additionally they rarely work in isolation, benefiting from bouncing ideas around with their peers. Students communicate freely about a peer's work, admitting that peer assessment is the best form of assessment. As mentioned above, feedback is essential to the creative process as it establishes the space in which the individual relates to his or her surrounding.

'I like (it) when people talk about my work.'

STUDENT

As the outcome of the course depends largely on personal input, assessment becomes very personal.

Within this section students demonstrate a very confident approach. They build this through self-awareness, continuously constructing and assessing personal challenges. Students demonstrate:

- Passion and involvement
- Enjoyment, openness and wonder
- Seriousness and intention
- Multi-sensory approach to learning
- Climate of relaxed attention

Creativity guidelines

- Visual research as a more advanced brainstorming aid to mind association.
- Personal approach to the educational challenge.
- Foundation year as a preparation phase to an open creative mode.
- Objective and frequent feedback from peers.
- Space for interpretation within briefing.
- During the course students are guided through different materials, alien fields in which they need to adapt.
- Engineers work with a lot of known quantities... the ignorant approach can be quite inventive.
- Critique modelling a process in front of a student.

Professional skills and attitudes for engineering students

CYNTHIA MITCHELL, CAROLINE BAILLIE AND SIMON DEWULF

The case:
Second year chemical engineering students.
Design of a food processing laboratory practical,
University of Queensland
The research:
Videoconference with students and tutors
Focus discussion students
Reflective writings students
Open ended questionnaire students
Interview with lecturer

Creativity guidelines
Problem redefining
Open-endedness of the problem
Idea development stages
Use of videoconference and stimulated recall for reflection on learning
Enhance creative productivity within the constraints of academia
Constructive criticism – peer criticism
Reflective writing assessment
Assessing the sharing of knowledge rather then the possession of knowledge
Connection to prior knowledge

Introduction

A chemical engineering course in professional skills has been developed at the University of Queensland. The course lecturer decided to make these key skills seem relevant to the students and to give them a real practical exercise which they had to present as a communication exercise. She also decided to encourage their creative abilities during this task. Hence they were asked to design a laboratory class which they themselves might have to take as part of their course. They had to prepare a bid to tender, to the funding sponsor.

Case study method

This case study was challenged by the remoteness of the project partner. It was considered most appropriate to hold a videoconference in which focused questions were put to the Australian students about their experiences on the course. This was later transcribed and analysed. Part of the students' assessment was a self reflection in writing and this together with open-ended questionnaires constituted the case study material. Students were asked to discuss the course and its assessment during the videoconference. A day later they reviewed the video.

This 'stimulated recall evaluation' resulted in a greater degree of self reflection than had been anticipated and many students 'saw the point' of the course at this stage, where they had not previously.

Warm-up

The design of the course relied on teamwork. In order to facilitate the initial group set-up, the students themselves formed the groups. A warm-up icebreaker was used to help teambuilding. Students were asked to design a craft with two pieces of A4 paper and four bits of adhesive tape to prevent an egg from breaking when dropped from a certain height.

Problem description

'The problem as given'

Design a food processing laboratory practical for second year chemical engineering students.

'The problem as understood'

The students were challenged to translate the above into a feasible workload. Several problems arose interpreting the focus of the practical as process-based rather than product-based. Leaning towards one product tended to settle a group onto one solution, limiting other creative options being found when rewriting the problem. Different ideas within the group members of what was required for the problem caused confusion. Open-endedness was difficult for many.

Students realised that not everything could be done unless the groupwork was set up effectively. Each team was divided into three subteams: analysts (application experts), experimentalists and product marketers. This division spread the load, although communication problems arose between the subteams.

Idea development

Each group met several times a week to share their progress. Several team-check assignments were to be written, reflecting the team's activities. The feedback on team-checks assisted the direction of the groups' research. At this point, the tutor's experience was required to give appropriate feedback. If this feedback was too directed, students became even more confused. A conceptual barrier was the product/process interface. Students felt they were led astray – some tutors giving them the impression that a product was the most important outcome.

Properties of materials could be found in the literature or on the internet, although the literature on food processing is fairly limited. The groups were assisted by two postgraduate tutors. Several students interviewed existing companies, to bring in the 'real life' dimension. As information was scarce, most of the work involved pilot trials on setting up experiments and doing laboratory trials.

The experimental work was limited by the availability of equipment and students became aware of the need to be creative within constraints.

Teamwork

In managing the fixed time period, the teams were challenged by communication and working effectively as groups. A lot of time in the early stages was considered unproductive. The workload needed to be shared properly in order to match the given deadlines. There was also a danger of students spending too much time on this compared to other assignments.

Within the groups criticism versus cooperation set human barriers to overcome. Leadership and the subdivision of specialised groups tended to prevent confidence and fluid interaction between the group members. Courage is needed to be creative and to be laughed at. Good facilitation was required at all times as students were not used to working in this way.

"The course was also seen as being about learning how to take criticism."

STUDENT

Creative moves

Working within boundaries gave an opportunity to create alternative solutions. Contrary to student expectations, ignorance in the field allows a fresh look at the matter. Problem solving which already has a known solution becomes an exercise. Here students encountered a problem that hadn't been solved before, which gave space for creative solutions.

"You have got to be open for new ideas."

STUDENT

Guest lecturers were invited to discuss related issues and this was well appreciated. It brought new perspectives to the problem.

Reflective writing and assessment tasks

'Knowing what the lecturer is aiming at in assessments' and 'being steered in a particular direction' were experienced as constraints towards creativity. By assessing creativity the process is affected.

In the main report of their laboratory exercise, students were assessed on 'creativity'. They found this difficult to understand and the tutor found this hard to assess without feedback from students about their intentions. This was partially addressed by asking students to self-reflect on their work in a written document. Again, tutors found these hard to mark and in some cases feedback sounded a little like counselling. Students also found it hard to imagine how their thoughts and reflections could be assessed. They did however seem to take well to this chance for self expression and it provided a valuable way of exploring how each individual was thinking.

Taken together, the report and self-reflective document, in discussion with all tutors and students, seemed to provide an optimal process. The videoconference method to evaluate the case became an important part of this self-reflection. Students came to a focus group the following day and the very fact that people in the UK showed interest, and seeing and hearing themselves discuss the course, helped the self-reflection process enormously.

Creativity guidelines

- Problem redefinition: creativity at the stage of interpreting the problem.
- Encouraging diversity was helped by the open-endedness of the problem – a very different approach to what students were used to in most engineering subjects.
- Idea development stages in the project.
- Use of videoconference and stimulated recall for reflection on learning. This unusual technique has shown to be successful in stimulating greater interest in the reflective learning of the course.
- Development of approaches to enhance creative productivity within the constraints of academia.
- Use of constructive criticism and how to interpret peer criticism.
- Use of reflective writing for student assessment.
- Assessing the sharing of knowledge rather than the possession of knowledge. The course emphasised the process of sharing knowledge through the process of the group exercise.
- Connection of prior knowledge in the field. As students had virtually no background in food processing, they were allowed to draw on their own previous experience. The importance of this step was shown to be vital for sustaining their new experiences.

Modelling the case studies

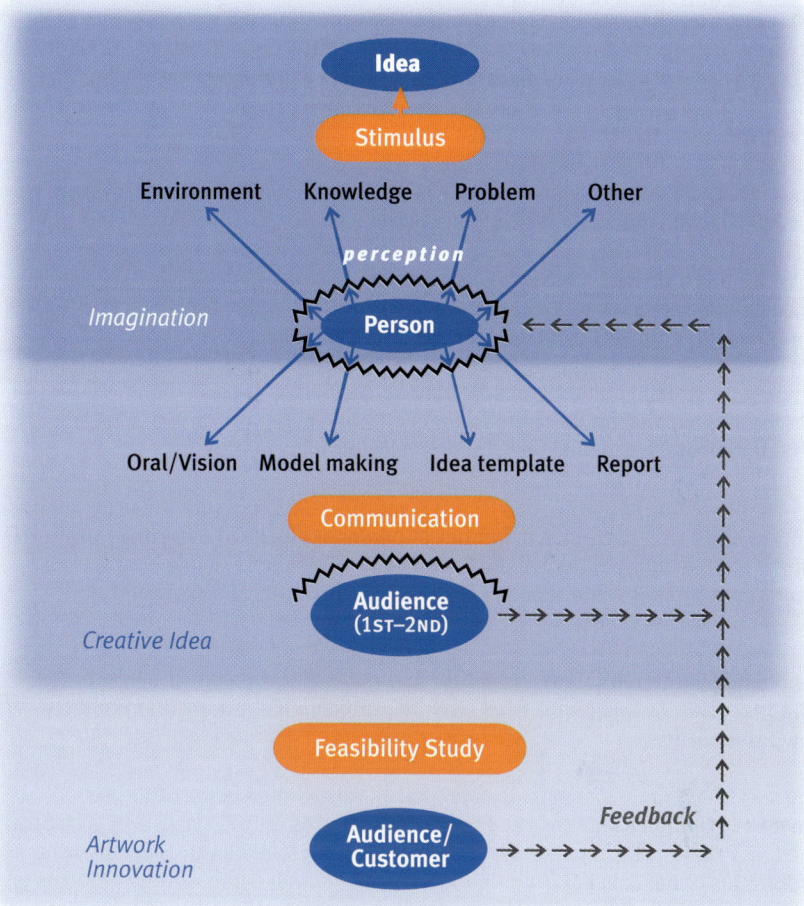

The model above represents the creative process from a personal perspective. It aims to structure the various routes individuals have taken, along with the five case studies. At any moment of the creative process, from preparation to verification, the individual will be stimulated to develop ideas, and communicate them to an audience.

As an individual, placed in an organisation (industrial or academic) we relate to the outside world through personal perception. These perceptions are influenced by several factors, which can act as filters or excitations to the individual, some of which have been discussed earlier. The individual may be intrinsically or extrinsically motivated. The **environment** is one possible stimulant. Group work falls into this category, as it becomes the environment in which our person is placed. Students working in an interactive setting with the possibility of group work will allow an individual to gain input from multiple perspectives, which is a healthy environment for individual creativity.

At university as well as when entering a new company the individual is exposed to new **knowledge**. This knowledge stream permits us to make new links, associating different facts, creating a new reality. This has proved to be a great stimulus for inventive thinking. New knowledge from different fields will always help to make new associations. The study of nature provides analogies in order to apply its principles to engineering concepts in an area known as biomimetics.

Defining the **problem** (and then redefining it) is a common way of initiating creative thinking. Problem setting is approached in different ways, sets of ideas in a similar fashion to the reformulation technique at the start of a creative process.

We can guide our potential idea through various stimuli. Before initiating the idea in one's mind we experience a number of personal blocks to overcome. Up to this point we demonstrate creative potential. This will result in 'being creative' as soon as we communicate the idea to an external party and transcend from imagination to creativity.

We bounce our potential idea to a first audience. The communication process here is crucial. At this point ideas may be protected as 'intellectual property' at a patent office.

One successful route for communicating ideas was studied in the BOC case – **the idea template**. Its success has been demonstrated in BOC Gases and is largely due to its democratic, ergonomic property (no hierarchical block). The idea-owner outlines his or her concept in written form on an internal database. The proposal is then examined by a team of gatekeepers, to discuss its potential.

Whether we are attempting to present our idea verbally or in any other way, we are at risk of various barriers. The audience can experience conceptual, hierarchical or cultural blocks, and it becomes a great challenge to us to direct them to the concept. These internal and external barriers and ways of overcoming them were discussed in the creative potential section. Classical critics will pursue the devil's advocate attitude to the best of their abilities to stall the idea. Here the self-confidence and positive stubbornness of the idea-owner will play a great part. Techniques to develop skills to overcome these barriers have also been previously discussed.

If possible, we will follow the route of making a scale model or pilot to ultimately convince the audience. At this point large numbers of ideas are lost, as we do not possess the time or courage to complete this process. In a university the conflict between time required to innovate in our teaching versus that needed for research will be a major stumbling block.

If the process is successful, we face the challenge of developing the 'creative idea' into an innovation, invention or piece of artwork.

Now we are faced with a second audience, which may be the customer. It may well be the hosting institution, whether this is industrial or academic. The person will undertake a market search to identify a target application and a feasibility study. A financial study to obtain the necessary components will require outside support. Again we will be facing blocks involving cost, time, and so on.

The greatest reward we will receive at the end of the process is the recognition of a potential idea, initiated in our own brain.

Implementing 'creativity' in an educational context

CAROLINE BAILLIE, SIMON DEWULF, PAUL WALKER AND LEWIS ELTON

Introduction

So far we have explored the literature for ideas about what creativity might be, we have studied it, we have presented cases where creativity seems to be inspired and we have focused in each case on the process of an individual taking an idea through the path of creative development. It was the intention of this book to take our reader through this path of learning, rather than present a 'fait accompli' in order that some of the ways of thinking, as well as the excitement and intrigue of creativity might be engendered. In this section, we come back to our original aim, and that is to find ways of fostering creativity in engineering students within an engineering curriculum. By now, however, it is evident that many of the ideas generated in this book are taken from, and relevant to, any area we wish to develop in a creative way.

In this section we will firstly take a very brief look at the education literature on related issues, we will then return to our case studies and take a fresh look at the guidelines or principles, which have been highlighted in each case. We will apply them to our creative process model, which will embed them in the literature and finally endeavour to put them into the context of a traditional engineering curriculum by providing examples of implementation of ideas.

Teaching, learning and assessing

Education comes from the root *educere*, to draw out or to lead, but many have grown up with the meaning 'to stuff in' (Gelb, 1996). As is apparent in the various case studies, the more appropriate approach for fostering creativity is experiential learning, where the teacher is a facilitator, through encouragement of the development of awareness by reflection, articulation and application of insight to real concepts. Such an approach is extensively documented in Brockbank and McGill (1988). It also links closely with developed conceptions of learning – where learning is described as 'changing as a person' (Marton *et al* 1993). Postman and Weingartner (in Cowan, 1998) argue that the ability to identify and ask good questions is the best measure of the quality of someone's education. 'Reflection is... the power acquired by a consciousness to turn in upon itself to take possession of itself, as an object endowed by its own particular consistence and value; no longer merely to know, but to know one's self, no longer merely to know but to know that one knows' (Cowan, 1998). This process of reflection could be described as the incubation stage, if we consider learning to involve 'creating' knowledge or understanding.

Creativity in a group

A recent paper by Baillie and Hession (1998) has explored the learning process in a problem based group learning environment, within the subject 'Global Environmental Change'. The learning processes were compared with Marton *et al's* six levels of individual learning (context nonspecific) as shown below:

Conception of learning in a group (Baillie and Hession, 1998)	Conceptions of learning as an individual (Marton *et al*, 1993)
6. Being creative	6. Changing as a person
5. Creative thinking	5. Seeing something in a different way
4. Proactive thinking	4. Learning as understanding
3. Elucidation	3. Learning as applying
2. Integrating diversity	2. Learning as reproducing
1. Functional	1. Increasing one's knowledge

Although there does not appear to be a great correlation at first sight, when we consider the learning context, we can see some parallels. If learning as an individual at its most simplistic, involves the 'doing' of expanding the number of facts in our brain, then learning in a group involves the 'doing' of working together in a team. As we move up the hierarchy (in which each level is inclusive of those below), we see that the descriptions of higher level learning involve 'seeing things in a different way, or 'creative thinking' and at best, changing as a person or 'being creative'.

Students learning in a group and describing learning in the latter category were able to see that they were using the experience of the multiple perspectives and personalities in the group to 'bring ideas from the back of their brain to the front' and their brains were 'firing on all four cylinders'. In the above study, the concept of global environmental change was explored by groups of students from different disciplines. This did appear to be a key factor in the development of their learning. When interviewed, the students who had the deepest approach expressed their experience of learning in ways that demonstrated they were 'creating' an understanding. They had changed in their ability to see from a variety of perspectives. This issue of variation appears to be the key to the essence of creativity in a group or the inspiration of creativity by working in a team.

The issue of variation or learning from different perspectives is the basis of the learning theory proposed by Bowden and Marton (1998) who propose that students learn when they are exposed to other students' ways of understanding something.

Developing new ways of seeing (situations, phenomena) is, of course, not the only form of learning, but it is the most fundamental and neglected form of learning. The reason is that once we have developed certain ways of seeing, they become taken for granted: we believe that what we see is the world as it is, and not the world as it is seen by us. We all take our ways of seeing the world for granted and we see it differently from each other, mostly without being aware of these differences. This is perhaps the most serious dilemma of the university when it comes to developing knowledge, which is new for individuals – through teaching and studying – or knowledge, which is new in an absolute sense – through research. Knowledge rests always on particular ways of seeing the world and usually we are not even aware of them. When the different ways of seeing are not shared, by teachers and students or by researchers representing somewhat different specializations, it is a most serious and often unseen problem. It is serious precisely because it is unseen. The relationship between learning and research is to be found here in its most profound sense; through the most important form of learning learners develop new ways of seeing and through the most important form of research new ways of seeing are introduced in our collective understanding of the world (p278).

By learning, we widen the range of possiblities of seeing the same thing. Our world grows richer and we have more options for our actions... To discern an aspect is to differentiate among various aspects and focus on the one most relevant to the situation. Without variation there is no discernment... Learning in terms of changes in or widening of our ways of seeing the world can be understood in terms of discernment, simultaneity and variation. Thanks to the variation, we experience and discern critical aspects of the situations or phenomena we have to handle and, to the extent that these critical aspects are focused on simultaneously, a pattern emerges.... Effective action springs from the way the situation is seen... (from focusing) on critical aspects of professional situations... The capability of discerning and focusing on critical aspects of situations and seeing the patterns characterizing those situations is a far more holistic capability than those commonly defined in competency-based approaches. Moreover, such holistic capabilities represent the links between disciplinary knowledge and professional skills. They are the results of the tranformation of the eyes through which the professional world is seen, brought about in, and by, the scholarly world. (pp7-8, 11-12)

There may be a way towards creativity in a group via problem based learning. However, the way is not obvious. All the evidence in the literature is that creativity in individuals has an unconscious element; it is that which leads to bisociation of ideas (juxtaposition of two seemingly unrelated ways of thinking) (Koestler, 1989). Could this unconscious element be replaced for groups at least in part by deliberate practice, such as, for example, brainstorming? If we want our students to incline towards creativity we should present them with primarily problem-oriented curricula, whatever subject they are studying. For some of these problems, the development of group skills which favour creative approaches should be main learning objectives and the problems must be formulated accordingly. This goes beyond the kind of problem based learning, common in medical education, which has in the main learning objectives in the cognitive and in the diagnostic skills domains (Little *et al*, 1995).

Creativity in a group therefore might be seen as a group creating something together by sharing ideas and perspectives (the main issue here would appear to be the necessity to 'share imagination', our working definition of creativity). The group environment might also be seen as the environment for healthy creativity within the individual who is inspired by these multiple perspectives.

Intelligence versus creativity

This topic is again highly debated in the literature although the main conclusion appears to be that which we would instinctively imagine – studies of intelligence from IQ scores and creativity show that highly creative people often have high IQs but individuals with high IQs are not necessarily highly creative (Ohara in Sternberg, 1999). It is anticipated that some people may be so highly rewarded for their high IQs – their analytical ability, that they fail to reach their creative potential within. Creative people are said to have high synthetic ability (can find problems, or create ideas, analytical skills (can evaluate these ideas) and practical skills (can communicate these ideas and persuade people of their value (Ohara in Sternberg, 1999)).

Knowledge versus creativity

Creativity has an interesting relationship with knowledge. Too much knowledge can stultify creativity but it is obvious that a knowledge base is required. Many studies of this area exist and it is proposed that higher levels of knowledge are associated with lower levels of eminence in studies of genius talent (Weisberg, 1999) and that there is a U-shaped relation between formal education and creativity. This is of course assuming that the function of formal education is to provide the individual with 'knowledge'. We might therefore propose moving from fact-based lectures to problem-based tutorials. However, this needs careful setting up. Studies on problem solving have shown that individuals can be induced to perform inefficiently in problem solving situations as a result of success with one specific solution. Students seem to look for a pattern in the solution rather than a pattern in the question.

Assessment versus the creative process

The Engineering Council UK suggest that requirements for a qualified engineering graduate should include creativity (SARTOR). However little guidance is given as to how this might be fostered or assessed. In the art environment, the usual platform for communication of a creative idea is through the 'crit' or critical appraisal. This is sometimes applied to the engineering culture through design studies but is mostly left to the architects and 'creative' designers. What could also possibly be transferred to engineering from the art world is the idea of assessing the strength of the concept separately from its execution as discussed in the Brighton case. Much literature abounds on self assessment and peer assessment in a formative manner as this helps students to reflect upon their own abilities and performance in certain tasks. They may be asked to mark work against a set of criteria (Cowan, 1998, Boud, 1986).

However, evaluation and effectiveness of creativity itself as an assessment criterion does not appear to have been widely documented in education literature even though it is an established criterion in many universities for gaining a fist class degree. The main area where creativity is 'tested' is within the psychometric domain. Mostly in the US, tests which assess student's ability in a range of tasks or 'paper and pencil' tests for creative potential (eg. Torrance in Sternberg, 1999) have been developed. These are often applied, alongside personality tests for divergent or convergent thinking 'types' to assess the success of various courses in fostering creativity in students.

The problems associated with assessment of creativity are that features associated with creativity and not creativity itself are often measured (ability to think laterally, adaptability, ability to synthesise etc). In the Queensland case it was found difficult to assess creativity in reports, without a discussion between students and tutors. It seems necessary for students to be allowed to defend their case as in a crit. The self-reflective essays in the Queensland case partially addressed this issue. It is imperative however that creativity is not made a criterion for marking unless this is properly understood by both students and staff and discussed in some way between them.

Key principles – how to foster creativity

The following table portrays the various creative guidelines drawn out from each case study. These principles have been collected together into a simple proforma, relating to the creative process, which they help to foster and indicated on the model shown previously. It is hoped that they will provide guidelines for ideas on how to foster creativity in many different courses, especially engineering. Some suggestions for implementation have been highlighted.

Stimulators – these are the various ways in which an individual with a particular motivation is stimulated to the generation of an idea.

Unblockers – These are categorised into preparation, generation, incubation and verification stages although it is appreciated that there will be a considerable amount of overlap which is not demonstrated in this simplistic analysis. These features of the cases which aid the creative process, can be seen as 'unblockers' and enable the individual to pass through the barrier or block to the idea, the creative idea or to the innovation, in the model. These pathways are indicated on the model.

Communicators – These are the ways in which the creative idea is communicated to the audience. It is a chance for feedback and reflection, redesign and further promotion of exploration and incubation in a cyclical manner.

Preparation
Prior knowledge
Problem setting
Freedom
Immersing into a way of thinking
Generation
Convergent/divergent thinking
Knowledge building
Personal development
Creativity techniques
Group/personal
Incubation
Verification
Student evaluation
Assessment

Stimulators
Motivation

Communicators
Ease of expression
Enthusiast

In the following descriptions the cases from which the principles are derived are given by the codes Brighton – B , University of Queensland – UQ , University College London – UCL , BOC , and Imperial College – IC . Ideas of ways in which to utilise the principles in an engineering or in any other higher educational context are given in the suggestion boxes.

Stimulus

Visual research (B)
Brainstorming sessions (IC)
Location/environment (UCL)
New knowledge (BOC)

> Visual research – ask students to collect together all manner of items which they can see, hear, feel etc which allow them to explore different perspectives and different ways of looking at their problem – a three dimensional brainstorming

Motivation

Extrinsic
Appraisal, rewards (BOC)
Intrinsic
Produce something – personal
ownership (B)
Intrigue (UCL)

> Reward innovation and creativity as part of student assessment and lecturer evaluation

Prior knowledge

Foundation year (B)
Unlearning – brainstorming (IC)
Question received view (B)
Connection to prior knowledge (UQ)

> Introduce brainstorms at the beginning of a lecture to bring students' knowledge to the front of their brains and for the lecturer to know what they need to 'unlearn'

Schneps (1994) has demonstrated in a very powerful video, 'A Private Universe', that facts are not sustainable when individuals are faced with contradicting prior knowledge. Students learn the concept without connecting with the prior knowledge. They reproduce the knowledge effectively during examination or assessment, after which they return to the prior concept. The problem arising here is that the new knowledge has never overwritten the previous version and is therefore not linked to the personal thinking of the individual.

Problem setting

Open-endedness (UQ , UCL , B)
Personal rather than content driven (B)
Briefings about the work (B)
Problem redefining (UQ)

> Set open-ended problems and ask students to discuss ideas after a short briefing. Allow the problem to be redefined and solved in very different ways

Freedom

Average or extraordinary (UCL , B)
Recognising our assumptions (B)
Company wide access (BOC)

Introduce a voluntary student group, run by students, as a club perhaps, in which they can take workshops in creative thinking and solve problems set by companies. These companies will gain excellent new ideas and will hopefully sponsor such a venture!

Immersing into a way of thinking

Intensive course (UCL , IC – Cairo)

Try to timetable all lectures of the 'creative' type together in a block to help maintain the necessary way of thinking

Convergent/divergent thinking

Left/right brain approaches combined (BOC , IC)

Satisfy all types of students by introducing a range of teaching and assessment tasks - some traditional, some innovative, some analytical closed problems, some open-ended

Knowledge building

Concept restructuring (IC)
Guided through new knowledge (BOC)

Revisit the course content and the way concepts are organised. Can they be logically ordered in a different way? Ask the students to create a mind map of how these concepts link together and to other parts of the course

Personal development

Handing over responsibility (UCL)
Developing awareness (all)
Personal journey (B)

> Give students tasks with increasingly more responsibility rather than expect them to take over on day one

Techniques

Learning skills, techniques (UCL)

> Although it is good for the students to apply their creative thinking skills to a problem in the context of their course, they may profit from learning some creative thinking techniques to apply to their problem solving

Group/person

Creativity in a group (UQ , UCL)
Personal creativity (B)

> It is important for the facilitator to develop an effective team in terms of safety, comfort and receptiveness of ideas. The important consideration for group members is that the unique perspective of all participants is encouraged and facilitated

Student evaluation

Self reflection (UQ)
Focus groups (IC , UQ , UCL)
Video stimulated recall (UQ , UCL)

> Hold a small discussion group at the end of the course for formative feedback. Never trust just one method of feedback, especially closed or numerical tick box questions designed for traditional lectures. These will give little useful feedback

> Film students in action and play it back to them, so they can reflect on their learning

Assessment

Group crits (B)
Group reflection (UQ , UCL)
Mark strength of concept and execution
separately (B)
Self reflection (UQ , UCL , B)
Exams – learning hierarchy (IC)
Creativity criteria (IC)
Sharing rather than possession of
knowledge (UQ)

Ask students to write a reflective
analysis of their work - why they did
it the way they did, and mark it as
part of the assessment

Assess student ideas and concepts
separately from their execution eg. in
projects and case studies

Group 'crits' could be used for
design studies or poster projects

Ease of expression

Idea template (BOC)
Visual research (B)
Feedback (UQ , B , BOC)
Idea development (UQ , BOC , UQ)

Consider a web-based computer
template for students to download
creative ideas at the university -
where else can they develop their
ideas into innovations?

Enthusiast

Innovation Director (BOC)
Facilitators (IC , UCL , UQ)

Try to find an enthusiast who will
generate motivation in others.
Someone who genuinely believes in
creativity. There are lots around...

References

Abra, J. (1997). *The Motives for Creative Work,* Hampton Press Cresskill, New Jersey

Bentley, T. (1997). *Sharpen Your Team's Skills in Creativity,* University Press, Cambridge

Baillie, C.A., Hession, M. (1998). *Global Environmental Change,* presented at Improving Student Learning Conference, Brighton

Baillie, C. (1999). *Learning from Nature,* Wissenschaftkolleg, unpublished, Berlin

Boden, M.A. (ed) (1996). *Dimensions of Creativity,* The MIT Press, London

Bohm, D., Nichol L. (eds) (1998). *On Creativity.* Routledge, London

Boud, D. (1986). *Implementing Student Self-Assessment,* Herdsa, Australia

Bowden, J., Marton, F. (1998). *The University of Learning: Beyond Quality and Competence in Higher Education,* Kogan Page Ltd, London

Brockbank, A., McGill, I. (1998). *Facilitating Reflective Learning in Higher Education,* SRHE and Open University Press, Buckingham

Buzan, T. (1999). *The Mindmap Book,* BBC Books, London

Clemen, R.T. (1996). *Making Hard Decisions: An Introduction to Decision Analysis,* Duxbury Press

COCD, (1994), *Creaddenda – Deskundigheids opleiding,* COCD, Antwerp

Cowan, J. (1998). *On Becoming an Innovative University Teacher,* SRHE and Open University Press, Buckingham

Eysenck, H.J. (1996). The Measurement of Creativity. In Boden, M.A.(ed) *Dimensions of Creativity,* The MIT Press, London

Finke, R.A., Ward, T.B., Smith, S.M. (1992). *Creative Cognition: Theory, Research and Applications,* The MIT Press, London

Gardner, H. (1982). *Art, Mind and Brain: A Cognitive Approach to Creativity,* Basic Books

Gelb, M.J. (1996). *Putting your Creative Genius to Work: How to sharpen and Intensify your Mind Power*, Nightingale Conant, Illinois

Gilhooly, K.J. (1996). *Thinking: Directed, Undirected and Creative,* Academic Press ltd., London

Goldschmidt, V., ASME (1999). *Learning the Art of Engineering in Creativity Class,* http://www.asme.org/students/learning.html

Hohn, H., Verloop, J. (1998). *Fostering Creativity in Difficult Groups: Lessons from Practice,* ICN Newsletter, Vol. 4, Nr2

Isaksen, S.G., Murdock, M.C., Firestien, R.L. (eds) (1993). *Nurturing and Developing Creativity: The Emerge of a Discipline,* Alex Publishing Corporation, New Jersey.

Isaksen, S.G., Murdock, M.C., Firestien, R.L. (eds) (1993). *Understanding and Recognizing Creativity: The Emerge of a Discipline,* Alex Publishing Corporation, New Jersey

Koestler, A. (1989). *The Act of Creation,* Penguin Books, London

Little, P., Ostwald, M., Ryan G (eds) (1995) *Research and Development in Problem Based Learning,* Charles Sturt University Press, Australia

Marton, F., Bealy, E., Dall'Alba, G. (1993). *Conceptions of learning, International Journal of Educational Research,* 19, 277-300.

Martin, J. (1998). *On Creativity: Fifteen ways to Leave your... Un-creativity,* http://www.concentric.net/~Jerbob1/cresub2.html

McKim, R.H., (1980). *Experiences in visual thinking,* PWS Publishing Company, Boston

Petty, G., (1997). *How to be better at... Creativity,* Kogan Page Ltd, London

Robinson, G., Rundell, J. (eds) (1994). *Rethinking imagination: Culture and creativity,* Routledge, London

Russell, N.C., (1998). *Learning, thinking and creating in Science and Technology: Creative Thought, MSc Science Communication,* Imperial College, London

Schneps, M.H. (1994). *A Private Universe,* The Corporation for Public Broadcasting, Massachusetts

Sternberg, R.J. (ed) (1997). *The Nature of Creativity: Contemporary psychological perspectives,* Cambridge University Press

Sternberg, R.J. (ed) (1999). *Handbook of Creativity,* Cambridge University Press

Tomic, W., Brouwers, W., (1998). *Idea Generating Among Secondary School Teachers.* The Open University (unpublished) Heerlen, The Netherlands

Ward, T.B., Finke, R.A., Smith, S.M. (1995). *Creativity and the Mind: Discovering the Genius within,* Plenum Press, London

Ward, T.B., Finke, R.A., Vaid, J. (eds) (1997). *Creative thought: An Investigation of Conceptual Structures and Processes,* American Psychological Association, Washington

Weisberg, R.W. (1999). *Creativity and Knowledge: A Challenge to Theories.* In Sternberg, R.J. (ed) (1999). Handbook of Creativity, Cambridge University Press

Acknowledgements

Caroline and Simon would like to thank everyone who has spent hours with one or both of them in coffee shops, cafés, pubs, trains and restaurants, getting inspiration for this book. 'CASE' is the product of a DfEE funded project, 'Fostering Creativity within Engineering' and the support of the DfEE is very much appreciated. Their recognition of such an important area of education and employment allowed studies to take place which would not otherwise have found time or incentive.

Thanks must go most of all to the project partners, the project steering committee and the Enthusiasts' Network, especially Tony Claydon, Alison Ahearn, Chris Wise and Nick Russell. The project came out of discussions with all five partners over a period of several months, with the excited anticipation of knowing that we were discovering a whole new world. It is hard to imagine anything now that is not 'generated' and 'incubated' because that is indeed what happened. Cynthia Mitchell, from the University of Queensland sowed the first seeds, in a sunny Dorset garden. The inspiration provided by Caroline's mother's roses was enough to launch what turned into the most exceptional, exhausting and exhilarating project ever. Paul Walker from University College London and Bas Sajik from BOC provided yet more innovative ideas, whilst Chris Rose of the University of Brighton, with sketching pencil always to hand, brought art to science and engineering with an understandable, stimulating and incredibly insightful perspective. Dave Clarke of Rolls-Royce supported us with an industry viewpoint, donating precious time to help us provide a user guide that would aid the development of the sorts of graduates Rolls-Royce might want to employ. And finally thanks to Lewis Elton, our favourite steering committee member, who guided us with his wisdom in what works and what doesn't in higher education.